ROUGH GUIDES

T0085813

POCKET **ROUGH GUIDE**

SNOWDONIA
& NORTH WALES
WEEKENDER

YOUR TAILOR-MADE TRIP
STARTS HERE

Tailor-made trips and unique adventures crafted by local experts

Rough Guides has been inspiring travellers with lively and thought-provoking guidebooks for more than 35 years. Now we're linking you up with selected local experts to craft your dream trip. They will put together your perfect itinerary and book it at local rates.

Don't follow the crowd – find your own path.

HOW ROUGHGUIDES.COM/TRIPS WORKS

STEP 1

Pick your dream destination, tell us what you want and submit an enquiry.

STEP 2

Fill in a short form to tell your local expert about your dream trip and preferences.

STEP 3

Our local expert will craft your tailor-made itinerary. You'll be able to tweak and refine it until you're completely satisfied.

STEP 4

Book online with ease, pack your bags and enjoy the trip! Our local expert will be on hand 24/7 while you're on the road.

BENEFITS OF PLANNING AND BOOKING AT ROUGHGUIDES.COM/TRIPS

PLAN YOUR ADVENTURE WITH LOCAL EXPERTS

Rough Guides' English-speaking local experts are hand-picked, based on their experience in the travel industry and their impeccable standards of customer service.

SAVE TIME AND GET ACCESS TO LOCAL KNOWLEDGE

When a local expert plans your trip, you save time and money when you book, even during high season. You won't be charged for using a credit card either.

MAKE TRAVEL A BREEZE: BOOK WITH PEACE OF MIND

Enjoy stress-free travel when you use Rough Guides' secure online booking platform. All bookings come with a money-back guarantee.

WHAT DO OTHER TRAVELLERS THINK ABOUT ROUGH GUIDES TRIPS?

Trip to Spain

This Spain tour company did a fantastic job to make our dream trip perfect. We gave them our travel budget, told them where we would like to go, and they did all of the planning. Our drivers and tour guides were always on time and very knowledgable. The hotel accommodations were better than we would have found on our own. Only one time did we end up in a location that we had not intended to be in. We called the 24 hour phone number, and they immediately fixed the situation.

Don A, USA ★★★★★

Trip to Morocco

Our trip was fantastic! Transportation, accommodations, guides – all were well chosen! The hotels were well situated, well appointed and had helpful, friendly staff. All of the guides we had were very knowledgeable, patient, and flexible with our varied interests in the different sites. We particularly enjoyed the side trip to Tangier! Well done! The itinerary you arranged for us allowed maximum coverage of the country with time in each city for seeing the important places.

Sharon, USA ★★★★★

PLAN AND BOOK YOUR TRIP AT ROUGHGUIDES.COM/TRIPS

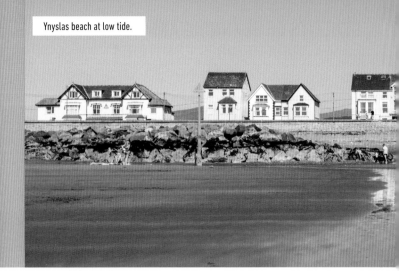

Ynyslas beach at low tide.

CONTENTS

Things not to miss

From its rugged mountains, dark forests and glorious coastlines to its medieval castles, slate caverns and vintage railways, here are the top attractions of this beautiful corner of Wales.

∧ **Blaenau Ffestiniog and Slate Caverns.** Atmospheric Victorian village high in the mountains, where visitors can go deep underground to explore the slate caverns. See page 47.

∧ **Snowdon.** This iconic mountain is the highest peak in both England and Wales, and a magnet for climbers and hill walkers. See page 56.

∧ **Centre for Alternative Technology.** This fascinating centre may date back to the 1970s, but it now seems extremely modern, with its focus on green ways of living. See page 94.

> **Portmeirion.** Fantasy Italianate village created by Clough Williams-Ellis and which featured in the original cult TV series, *The Prisoner*. See page 71.

National Slate Museum. Discover the story of the Welsh slate industry at this museum located in former Victorian workshops. See page 55.

Llandudno. This Victorian seaside resort is one of the jewels of North Wales, with a fine promenade, pretty gardens and some good shops. See page 18.

Ffestiniog Railway. This nineteenth-century narrow-gauge railway started life carrying slate through the Welsh mountains, but now gives tourists a wonderfully scenic journey. See page 45.

Caernarfon. While best known for its magnificent castle, Caernarfon is also a busy holiday town with plenty of attractions and places to eat and drink. See page 51.

Harlech. Harlech's castle dominates the hillside town and overlooks a gloriously unspoilt swathe of sandy beach that is ideal for families. See page 72.

Conwy. Charming little town with a mighty castle and well-preserved medieval walls, Conwy makes a lovely base for exploring. See page 19.

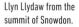
Llyn Llydaw from the summit of Snowdon.

INTRODUCTION TO
Snowdonia and North Wales

The craggy mountains and green valleys of North Wales combine to produce some of the most dramatic, and wildest, landscapes in Britain. At their heart is Snowdonia.

When the traveller and essayist George Borrow toured North Wales in 1854, he wrote: 'Perhaps in all the world there is no region more picturesquely beautiful.' A bold claim, yet one not hard to justify – and one that is

surely shared by thousands of visitors today. Elsewhere there may be loftier mountains, deeper lakes, greater forests and swifter rivers but rarely are they found in such unique combinations.

Today, while Welsh Black cattle and the ubiquitous Welsh Mountain sheep share their hillsides with walkers and cyclists, climbers and hang-gliders, farming continues much as it has for generations. Dry-stone walls snaking over ridge and summit date from the eighteenth and nineteenth centuries, separating valley from *ffridd* (mountain pasture), one farm from the next.

North Wales may not boast the sunniest weather in Britain, but it might well boast some of the cleanest air, the most pristine countryside, the strongest sense of history – oh,

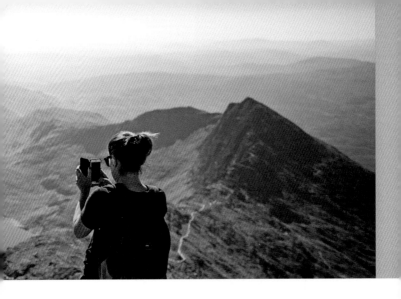

and some of its loveliest beaches. It is undoubtedly a green haven for lovers of the outdoors, especially the northwest corner known as Snowdonia. Eryri's peaks are a thrilling presence: inspirational to explore by road, challenging to those who walk and climb. The great crags and gullies have become associated with Britain's best-known rock climbers and mountaineers. The northeast corner is less dramatic, but contains some gloriously unspoilt villages, pretty market towns and sublime, pastoral scenery.

Location and topography

Igneous rock along with volcanic ash, lava and shale from the Ordovician Period makes up much of the savagely beautiful geology around Snowdon and Cadair Idris. Older Cambrian rocks are most evident in the mountains of the Harlech Dome bordering Tremadog Bay. But by far the most striking influence on the entire Snowdonia landscape has been that of glacial ice.

The Ice Age which began some 2 million years ago and ended

Hiking up Snowdon.

Storm clouds gather over the mountains.

around 10,000 years ago has left an extraordinary and highly visible legacy in Snowdonia. At times throughout that period of very cold climate cycles, great ice sheets thousands of feet thick spread from Scandinavia to Britain. Meanwhile, permanent accumulations of snow on higher ground spawned glaciers which slowly flowed downhill, grinding away the bedrock, smoothing out U-shaped valleys and depositing huge mounds of excavated material called moraines. Steeply hollowed basins known in Wales as *cwms*, usually now filled by lakes and surrounded by cliffs, were left behind in higher locations. The result is a mountain landscape little changed since the last glacier melted.

Climate

Hills and mountains create their own weather. Okay – it's wet. In common with most of upland Britain, there is greater rainfall (snow in winter) here than over the adjacent lowlands. More than 185in (4700mm) of precipitation have been recorded on the Snowdonia mountains in one year and even in a drought year 100in (2540mm) is not uncommon. Temperature falls as altitude is gained – about 5°F (3°C) for every 1000ft (305m). Snow often lingers on north-facing slopes above 2000ft (610m) well into May. Winds are notoriously fickle, sometimes funnelling viciously through valleys and over passes, at other times disappearing altogether in sheltered locations.

Snowdonia's climate – essentially a collection of mini-climates – is changeable throughout the year, with the best of the weather usually, though not always, to be found on the fringes of the hills. Higher villages and roads may be shrouded in mist for days

Centre for Alternative Technology.

Welsh slate

Much of Snowdonia's earlier prosperity rested upon slate: that impervious, blue-grey stone that splits so conveniently into flat sheets. The industry faded in the late nineteenth century and long-abandoned slate quarries still scar many a mountainside, particularly around Blaenau Ffestiniog, Bethesda and Llanberis. However, their narrow-gauge railways and workings have long become visitor attractions in their own right. High-quality slates are still produced in limited quantities and are much-prized by designers.

Llechwedd Slate Caverns at Blaenau Ffestiniog.

on end while those in the lee of high ground bask in sunshine. In westerly or southwesterly weather, districts such as the Vale of Conwy and the North Coast are often fine while the West Coast and most of the mountains sulk under cloud and rain. Similarly, east winds produce favourable conditions over Anglesey and the Lleyn.

May, June and September are the driest months in an average year.

Economy

Earning a living from the land in the rugged heart of Snowdonia has never been easy. Only the hardy Welsh Mountain sheep and Welsh Black cattle are able to withstand the harsh climate and convert rough grazing into profit for the farmer. Lambing extends from March well into April, after which each ewe and lamb will be driven up the hillside to range over its acre or so of ground. Shearing takes place during June and July.

While traditional agriculture continues in the more fertile valleys and lowland fringes, forestry and electricity generation (hydro, nuclear and wind power) contribute their share of regional income. In 2017 the Welsh Government promoted the strategy 'Moving North Wales Forward' to improve transport links and infrastructure in the area and promised investment to further grow such industries such as pharmaceuticals, aeorospace and technology. It is hoped this will keep young people in the region, thus keeping alive the Welsh culture and language for the next generation.

Environment

The windy, high ground of North Wales makes it an obvious choice for the siting of onshore wind farms – particularly as much of the area is sparsely populated, and land is relatively cheap. The Welsh Assembly, keen to create a low carbon economy and 'green' jobs, wants to more than double the energy it currently generates from onshore wind farms. Visitors will certainly be aware of their presence, the nature of which divides opinion in both Wales and the UK as a whole: some see them as clean, green and harmless, others as noisy eyesores that can have a negative effect on birdlife.

Food and Drink

You can eat practically anything you want in North Wales, especially in large settlements such as Caernarfon, which offers everything from Thai cuisine to traditional teas. You certainly won't go hungry, as portions tend to be generous. In recent years there has been a move to put local produce on menus, and this is worth seeking out – especially as it is often high quality and organic.

You have a wide choice of places to dine in North Wales – from hotels and restaurants with rooms, to neighbourhood restaurants, cafés and bistros. And don't forget the pubs, many of which serve good food and are particularly popular for Sunday lunch.

Welsh dishes

North Wales is justly proud of its succulent mountain-bred lamb and black beef, as well as salt-marsh lamb that is reared around Harlech. However, many visitors also savour the region's seafood. The Conwy Estuary and Menai Strait, both shallow and strongly tidal, provide ideal conditions for the cultivation of mussels, delicious served in a white wine and cream sauce, while the rocky shores around Anglesey and the Lleyn Peninsula yield excellent oysters, crabs and lobsters. For colder days try *cawl*, a traditional meat, root vegetable and leek soup; or perhaps *lobscows*, a warming lamb broth.

Fresh local vegetables, including the iconic Welsh leek, are widely available, and there are some delicious Welsh cheeses to try. The latter are produced in the south and west of the country, rather than the mountainous north, but are well worth seeking out – particularly some of the soft goat's cheeses. The best-known Welsh cheese is crumbly Caerphilly. Cheese features in a number of Welsh dishes, such as Glamorgan sausages (made from vegetables, herbs and cheese), and Welsh rarebit, a tasty mix of cheese, mustard and ale that is then grilled on toast.

Snowdonia specialities

Different parts of Snowdonia have their own products: organic meats from the Rhug Estate at Corwen and Cadwalader's celebrated ice cream (which originated at Criccieth in the 1920s but is now widely available) are just two examples. Then there is Halen Môn salt, a sea salt from Anglesey that is highly praised by top chefs. Morning coffee and afternoon tea provide opportunities to enjoy griddle-cooked Welsh cakes *(cacen radell)* which are flat, circular, fruited and spread with butter or caster sugar. Another teatime favourite is *bara brith*, a fruited tea bread.

The great Liberal politician and statesman David Lloyd George, who lived near Criccieth, relished simple Welsh country fare. Traditional recipes compiled by the Criccieth

A bowl of fresh mussels at the Gwledd Conwy Feast.

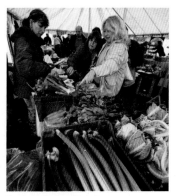

Llandudno Farmers' Market.

Farmers' markets

Going to a farmers' market is a great way to meet local people, as well as to pick up fresh local produce. They are held all over North Wales, some weekly (like that held each Thursday in Colwyn Bay), others monthly such as Anglesey's (Menai Bridge) and Dolgellau's (Eldon Square), the third Saturday and Sunday of each month respectively, and Mold's (St Mary's Church Hall) on the first and third Saturday of each month.

Women's Institute and first published after World War I included Steamed Snowdon Pudding under 'Recipes for the Favourite Dishes of the Prime Minister' section.

Welsh beer, wine and whisky

Beer is still the traditional alcoholic drink in Wales, the main brewery, Brains, is based in Cardiff in the south. To sample a real North Wales beer, look out for Purple Moose beers, which are brewed from an independent brewery in Porthmadog. The landscape

Halen Môn - Anglesey Sea Salt.

of the north is unsuited to vine growing; however, there are vineyards in South Wales where viticulture dates back to Roman times. Cariad Wines, from Llanerch, and Tintern, Parva Wines, from Tintern are the producers of some increasingly acclaimed whites. Also look out for Welsh mead, a fermented 'honey wine' made with honey and water: it's sweet – and often unexpectedly potent. A surprising addition to the Welsh drinks market came in the year 2000 when Penderyn distillery opened near the Brecon Beacons in South Wales; they've recently opened another distillery in Llandudno. It produces several single malt whiskies, as well as a Brecon Botanicals gin, a Brecon vodka and Merlyn Cream Liqueur. It's certainly worth seeking out in specialist stores.

Find our recommended restaurants at the end of each Tour. Below is a Price Guide to help you make your choice.

Eating out price guide

Two-course meal for one person, including a glass of wine.
£££ = over £30
££ = £15–30
£ = under £15

Conwy valley.

TOUR 1

The North Coast and Carneddau Mountains

This tour, which takes you from the pastoral Vale of Clywd to the heart of Snowdonia, is around 87.5 miles (140.5km) long and is ideally done over two days.

Lying beneath the Clwydian Hills is the lush Vale of Clywd, a pretty corner of Wales that tends to attract few tourists – despite being dotted with charming villages and historic churches. This tour starts here, in the market town of Ruthin, then sweeps down to the lively resorts of the north coast, where the A55 speeds you on to Llandudno, one of Britain's finest Victorian seaside resorts.

Further on you drive through the beautiful Vale of Conwy, a gentle landscape of fields and woodland leading to the darker conifers of Gwydir Forest and tumbling rivers around Betws-y-coed.

Later, your route takes you by the Carneddau mountains, described by

Highlights

- Ruthin
- St Asaph Cathedral
- Llandudno
- Conwy
- Betws-y-coed
- Capel Curig
- Llyn Ogwen

Thomas Pennant, in his famous *Tour in Wales* published in 1778, as 'very disagreeable, of dreary bottoms or moory hills...' Tastes change and many hillgoers now choose these sprawling whalebacks to escape the crowds on Snowdon and other popular peaks. Few

Get crafty

Make sure you pay a visit to Ruthin Craft Centre (Park Road; www.ruthincraftcentre.org.uk; free), a contemporary purpose-built structure just outside the centre of town. It houses galleries, artists' studios, exhibition space and also has an excellent shop where you can find all manner of handmade crafts, ranging from jewellery to ceramics, created by local specialists.

Jeweller Marjorie Schick's first UK exhibition was held in the Craft Centre.

roads penetrate far into these remote northernmost hills of Snowdonia, yet on every side they are bounded by scenery of extraordinary contrasts.

The Vale of Clywd

Ruthin ❶, pronounced 'Rithin', is a charming market town in Denbighshire that sits at a strategic point on the River Clywd, and is brimming with Welsh history. Edward I built a castle here in the thirteenth century, which was later besieged by Owain Glyndwr (who burned most of the town as well), as part of his bid for an independent Wales. In the Civil War, the castle became a Royalist fortress, but was eventually surrendered to Parliamentary forces – that soon destroyed most of it. The ruins were eventually incorporated

Nantclwyd y Dre, Ruthin.

into a nineteenth-century castle, which is now a hotel.

The castle is reached via Castle Street, which is home to **Nantclwyd y Dre** (www.denbighshire.gov.uk; charge), the oldest timbered town house in Wales, which dates back to 1435. Furnished 'period' rooms are devoted to different ages of the town's history: there are Georgian and Jacobean bedrooms – the former with fine Chinese wallpaper – a Victorian schoolroom, and a hallway from 1942, plus a restored garden, dating back to the thirteenth century.

Notable amongst the town's historic buildings is **Ruthin Gaol** (Clwyd Street; www.denbighshire.gov.uk; charge). Although temporarily closed, the historic site is due to reopen in April 2024. Constructed in the seventeenth century, it was in use until 1916, then renovated and reopened as a visitor attraction in 2004. In Victorian times, a wing was built in the same style as Pentonville prison in London. You can see the cells, learn about the lives of the prisoners, what they ate and how they were punished. One 'star' prisoner was John Jones, known as the Welsh Houdini. He made a rope from his bedding to escape from Ruthin Gaol – but is said to have died of shock after being shot whilst on the run.

Bodelwyddan Castle.

Llanrhaedr

From Ruthin, pick up the A525, and drive north to the hamlet of **Llanrhaedr** ❷ in the Vale of Clwyd, which sits just on the left of the road. The church here, **St Dyfnog's**, is famed for its stained-glass Jesse Window, which was completed in 1544 and is considered to be the finest in Wales. The window depicts Christ's family tree, showing his ancestors as far back as Jesse, the father of King David. It was removed during the Civil War to save it from rampaging Parliamentarians.

St Dyfnog came here in the sixth century, and if you follow a path from the churchyard to the woods, you can still see the Holy Well in which he would stand all day as a penance. It was once known for its healing properties.

Denbigh

Continue on the A525, branching left onto the A543 to reach **Denbigh** ❸, a market town whose name translates as 'little fortress' in Welsh. The town was a medieval centre of Welsh power and a residence for the Welsh princes. When Dafydd ap Gruffudd led a revolt against the English Crown, Edward I unleashed his forces, and in

1282 took the town, captured Dafydd (who was later executed), and charged his commander Henry de Lacy to build a castle on the remains of the prince's stronghold. **Denbigh Castle** (www.cadw.gov.wales; charge), which sits on a hilltop above the town, is one of the largest in Wales; its most striking feature is a triple-towered gatehouse. The town walls were built at the same time as the castle. The castle fell into disrepair, and in the sixteenth century Elizabeth I's favourite, Robert Dudley, was granted a lease on it. However, after the Civil War the castle deteriorated further and is now largely ruined.

Just outside Denbigh, on the A543, is **Gwaenynog Hall** (tel: 01745 812066; June–Aug, by appointment; voluntary donation), the garden of which was the inspiration for Beatrix Potter's *The Tale of the Flopsy Bunnies*. With apple and pear trees, and large herbaceous borders, the garden is still much as it was when Beatrix Potter painted it.

St Asaph

Returning to the A525 and continuing north, you soon reach **St Asaph ❹**, which might look like a small town, but is actually a city thanks to its **cathedral** (High Street; www.stasaphcathedral. wales; free but donations welcome). Dating back to the thirteenth century, this is the smallest cathedral in Britain, and sits on a site that has been a place of worship since AD 560. The church is named after a local saint and similar nearby place names point to the area as a former religious settlement. Inside is a superb collection of Welsh Bibles, including one by William Morgan, who was the first person to translate the Bible into Welsh. Only 800 of these were ever produced. Morgan is said to be buried somewhere in the churchyard.

Bodelwyddan Castle

From St Asaph continue to join the busy A55 going west, to reach **Bodelwyddan Castle ❺** (www.warnerleisurehotels.co.uk/hotels/bodelwyddan-castle-hotel). Built in the nineteenth century, on the site of a much earlier structure, Bodelwyddan Castle is more stately home than castle and once belonged to the Williams family who made a fortune in lead mining. During World War I it became a recuperation camp, while part of the grounds was turned into an area for trench warfare training. After a period as a girls' school, Bodelwyddan was opened to the public in the 1980s. You can still admire the exterior of this listed building from the outside, but as a result of the Covid-19 pandemic, it now only functions as a private hotel, as part of the Warner Leisure group.

Opposite the castle, on the other side of the A55, is the **Marble Church** with its soaring spire. Built in the nineteenth century, it gets its name from the 13 different types of marble used in the interior. The churchyard contains the graves of World War I Canadian soldiers who had been billeted nearby. The majority died from the Spanish flu pandemic, but five were shot during the Kinmel Riot of 1919. Troops waiting to be sent

Llandudno seafront.

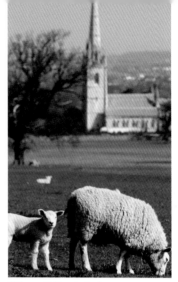

St Margaret's Church, also known as the Marble Church.

home had rebelled when their ship was diverted to Russia.

Continue driving west along the A55 and you soon reach Colwyn Bay, one of the waterfront resorts that dots this stretch of coastline. After a collapse of part of the famous Victorian pier in 2017, a newly built, albeit truncated, pier opened in 2021.

Llandudno

From Colwyn Bay rejoin the A55, continue west, then turn right on the A470 to reach **Llandudno ❻**, which lives up to its reputation as one of Britain's finest Victorian seaside resorts. Today grand hotels fronted by a broad promenade sweep round North Shore to the splendid Pier without an entertainments arcade or fast-food outlet in sight.

The town's early success prompted entrepreneurs to construct Marine Drive, a toll road encircling the Great Orme limestone headland which overlooks the town. It incorporates the **Bronze Age Great Orme Copper Mine** (www.greatormemines.

info; charge). The mines were first discovered in 1987, and archeologists gradually revealed a maze of tunnels dating back 4000 years. The highlight of the self-guided tour is the cavern, which was dug out using stone and bone tools. In 1902 a **Tramway** (www.greatormetramway.co.uk; charge) was laid to the Great Orme's 680ft (207m) summit in 1898, complemented, in 1969, by the Llandudno Cable Car (bit.ly/46t6bTm; charge), the longest in Britain. To savour this magnificent headland, walk round the perimeter wall from the car park, a distance of about 2 miles (3km); there are wide views over the Conwy Estuary to distant Anglesey, the Carneddau mountains and even the Isle of Man. The **Great Orme** is a country park and Site of Special Scientific Interest; its Visitor Centre (https://bit.ly/3M1fXUy) has a live camera link to enable visitors to watch local seabird colonies.

Llandudno Museum (Gloddaeth Street; www.llandudnomuseum.co.uk; charge) has a collection of bones dating back 14,000 years, which were found in Llandudno, together with prehistoric tools, Roman items (including a tile with a footprint embedded in it) and an exhibit on wartime Llandudno.

The town's many attractions include flowery walks through Haulfre and Happy Valley gardens, a dry ski slope and toboggan run, art exhibitions at **MOSTYN** (www.mostyn.org; free), a stunning contemporary art gallery, and prestigious productions at the **Venue Cymru** (www.venuecymru.co.uk), a theatre and conference centre on the seafront. There are also many independent shops, selling everything from clothes to ceramics. For Alice in Wonderland fans – Lewis Carroll and the Liddell family were frequent visitors to the town – pick up the Alice trail map from the tourist office in the library in Mostyn Street.

Conwy

Leave Llandudno on the A546, shadowing the River Conwy's eastern shore to Deganwy, and follow signs for Conwy, crossing the A55 tunnel approaches. On your left is Thomas Telford's Conwy Suspension Bridge, built in 1826 to replace the ferry and for many years the only vehicular

Llandudno for families

Llandudno is brimming with family-friendly attractions. For young ones there's a traditional Punch and Judy Show, held in summer on the North Shore Promenade. All ages should enjoy the underground tour at the Bronze Age Copper Mine on the Great Orme (especially considering the fact that some of the tunnels are thought to have been dug by children aged just 5 or 6). The whole family could also join a boat trip around the Great Orme. They take place daily from April to October (tel: 07833 498 557).

Punch and Judy show.

crossing. It is now pedestrianised with its tiny Toll House garden (tel: 01492 592246 for openings) restored in period style by the National Trust. Robert Stephenson's tubular railway bridge, opened 12 years later, runs alongside, carrying the main Euston to Holyhead line.

Enclosed by battlemented walls, **Conwy ❼** is one of the best preserved medieval fortified towns in Europe, and **Conwy Castle** (www.cadw.gov. wales/visit/places-to-visit/conwy-castle; charge) dominates arrival from the east. The castle was begun in 1283, contemporaneous with those at Harlech and Caernarfon, under the aegis of Edward I's talented military architect, James of St George. It took just four years to build. Allow time to explore the complex and to absorb its fascinating history in the adjacent Visitor Centre.

Nearly 1 mile (1.6km) in total length, with three gateways and 21 towers, **Conwy Town Walls** have survived almost unscathed. Walking along the ramparts reveals bird's-eye

Conwy's Town Walls.

views over nineteenth-century River Quay and the little town which boasts more than 200 buildings of special architectural interest. Notable among them is **Plas Mawr** (www.cadw.gov. wales/visit/places-to-visit/plas-mawr; charge), the finest Elizabethan town house in Britain. It was built for Welsh merchants, who obviously wanted to impress visitors with a display of elaborate plasterwork. There's also an atmospheric kitchen and courtyard

Conwy Castle.

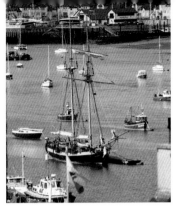

The view from Conwy Castle to Conwy Sands.

garden. Behind Plas Mawr is the **Royal Cambrian Academy of Art** (www.rca conwy.org; free) which exhibits the work of Welsh artists, while other attractions include **Aberconwy House** on Castle Street (tel: 01492 592246; www.nationaltrust.org.uk/visit/wales/aberconwy-house; charge), the town's only surviving medieval merchant's house, which is under the care of the National Trust – currently closed, there are plans to reopen it as a secondhand bookshop; and, down on the quayside, Britain's reputedly **Smallest House** (www.thesmallesthouse.co.uk; minimal charge), which has just two rooms, yet was inhabited until 1900 – by a fisherman who was over 6ft (1.8m) tall.

Vale of Conwy

Take the B5106 Trefriw road from the castle and follow it south along the pastoral **Vale of Conwy**. A mile (1.6km) past Ty'n-y-groes, poorly signed on the left, is a driveway to Caerhun, lowest fording point on the River Conwy since Roman times. It was guarded then by a fort – Canovium – in whose northeast quadrant sits the tiny medieval Church of St Mary. The site is also accessible by footpath from Tal-y-cafn bridge just over a mile (1.6km) to the north.

To the north of Dolgarrog, the B5106 passes along a broad reach of farmland before the Vale of

Conwy narrows to a flat flood plain at Trefriw. The village of Trefriw clings to a steep wooded hillside and straddles the Snowdonia National Park border. It is famed for a nearby chalybeate spring, which contains iron salts, and is believed to have been discovered by soldiers of the XXth Roman Legion. The Victorians, with a penchant for 'taking the waters', added a Pump Room and Bathhouse to the original ancient grotto, resulting in Trefriw Wells Spa becoming a major attraction.

Conwy's statue of Llewellyn the Great.

Go birding

Just outside Conwy is an RSPB Reserve (Llandudno Junction; www.rspb.org.uk), which has a visitor centre, café and hides where you can watch for birds such as lapwings. The site's extensive reed beds provide shelter for buntings and warblers, and you might also spot waders like the Black-tailed godwit. On Saturdays (late March–Dec) at 11am there are guided walks.

Above Trefriw lie two lakes, Crafnant and Geirionydd (both have encircling footpaths). Their waters flow down the Afon Crafnant to **Trefriw Woollen Mill** (www.t-w-m.co.uk; shop, tearoom and turbine house; weaving in operation mid-Feb–mid-Dec Mon–Fri), whose water turbines power the 1950s vintage mill machinery. Here you can see the weaving of traditional Welsh tapestries and tweeds, and possibly be able to try your hand at weaving on a small hand loom.

Llanrwst and Gwydir

Tortuous lanes to the west penetrate Gwydir Forest Park, a fascinating region of mine-scarred hills and secretive lakes. There are forest trails, picnic and car parking areas. Where the B5106 swings left, take the right fork for Betws-y-coed. The market town of **Llanrwst** ❽ lies just across the River Conwy, spanned by the graceful seventeenth-century three-arched bridge, Pont Fawr, which is attributed to Inigo Jones. The village church stands on a site once occupied by a sixth-century saint's cell. The neighbouring Gwydir Chapel is said to have been built by Inigo Jones and contains part of the coffin of Llewellyn ap Iowerth (Llewellyn the Great).

Off the first bend on the B5106 stands **Gwydir Castle** (www.gwydir castle.co.uk; charge), a Tudor mansion

The three-arched bridge over the River Conwy in Llanrwst, with the vine-clad National Trust property, Tu Hwnt-i'r-Bont, behind.

painstakingly restored following a fire in the 1920s and considered to be one of the most haunted houses in Wales. A family home (they offer bed and breakfast), the house contains a wood-panelled dining room – also attributed to Inigo Jones, who appears to have been busy in these parts – which was sold in 1921 to American press baron William Randolph Hearst and later passed to the New York Metropolitan Museum. The room was never unpacked, and in 1996 it was purchased and returned to Gwydir. Those seeking high-level adventure in the trees can visit **Zip World** (www.zipworld.co.uk; booking advisable; charge) by the A470, where visitors can enjoy a journey through the canopy on a Zip Safari, bounce on treetop nets, soar on a giant swing, whizz on a forest coaster or tackle the obstacle course. Just before joining the A5 at Betws-y-coed the road crosses Pont y Pair (Bridge of the Cauldron), from which intrepid (or maybe foolhardy) youngsters plunge on hot summer days.

Betws-y-coed.

Betws-y-coed

Situated at the eastern gateway to the Snowdonia National Park, **Betws-y-coed** ❾ (pronounced Betus-er-Quoid, and meaning 'Chapel in the Wood') is built around the confluence of three rivers, the Conwy, the Llugwy and the Lledr. Popular with Victorian honeymooners, and still a great base for exploring the area, the village was put firmly on the map by the Birmingham watercolourist, David Cox. Over the years the main street of greystone cottages and hotels has sprouted a rash of craft shops, outdoor equipment stores and eating places (see page 49). Several easy walks start here, particularly up to Llyn Elsi by the Jubilee Path, to forest-fringed Llyn y Parc, and along the River Llugwy to the Miners Bridge – all waymarked.

Betws has a station on the single-track **Conwy Valley Line** (www.conwyvalleyrailway.co.uk) running 27 miles/43km from Llandudno Junction to Blaenau Ffestiniog (see page 47) through stunning scenery. On the opposite

Capel Curig, in the northern half of the National Park.

side of the tracks, pop your head inside the sweet little **Conwy Valley Railway Museum** (www.conwy railwaymuseum.co.uk; charge), where you can also take a miniature train ride. Just behind here, and ignored by the crowds, sleeps the fourteenth-century St Michael's Old Church (www.stmichaelsbyc.org.uk; free),

Its convenient location adds to the Ogwen valley's popularity.

containing an effigy of Gruffydd ap Dafydd, great nephew of Llewellyn the Last, who fought in the wars of Edward III and the Black Prince.

Capel Curig

From Betws-y-coed the A5 climbs slowly to Swallow Falls, a beauty spot visited since the early nineteenth century where the Afon Llugwy drops 30ft (9m) into a deep pool, continuing as a single foaming torrent. Less than a mile (1.6km) ahead motorists pass Ty Hyll (The Ugly House), which dates from the Middle Ages and is owned by the Snowdonia Society (www.snowdonia-society.org.uk), featuring a teashop and honeybee exhibition, plus nature activities.

As **Capel Curig** ❿ is approached there are majestic views first of Moel Siabod (2861ft/872m) on the left, then to the Snowdon massif and the humpback Carneddau mountains. Capel Curig's equipment shops and friendly cafés serve the needs of the year-round outdoor fraternity, as does **Plas y Brenin** (www.pyb. co.uk), Wales's National Mountain Sports Centre, which runs courses in everything from hillwalking and navigation to skiing and sea kayaking.

Carnedd Llewelyn.

Carnedd Llewelyn

The highest summit in the Carneddau mountains, Carnedd Llewelyn (3,491ft/1064m), stands a mere 69ft (21m) lower than Snowdon itself. Carneddau means 'place of stones, or cairns', but while this describes the terrain here and there, grass predominates, swathing the vast ridges and cwms.

Llyn Ogwen

Five miles (8km) ahead beside Thomas Telford's London to Holyhead highway, pinched between the frowning Glyder and Carneddau peaks, lies **Llyn Ogwen** ⓫. Here, it is claimed, Sir Bedivere, last of Arthur's knights, cast Excalibur into the water. Llyn Ogwen is Snowdonia's shallowest lake with a mean depth of only 6ft (1.8m). Walk along the north-shore Fisherman's Path to appreciate the rearing bulk of Tryfan (3002ft/915m); its proximity to the A5 and its rocky ridges leading to twin summit boulders, christened Adam and Eve, attract large numbers of walkers. A path leading south from Ogwen Cottage to Cwm Idwal follows a rugged 2-mile (3km) nature trail revealing in graphic form the region's fascinating glacial origins, which attracted Charles Darwin in the nineteeenth century. Cwm Idwal is a Site of Special Scientific Interest – Arctic plants grow here, such as moss campion, saxifrages and even the insectivorous round-leaved sundew, which traps insects in its leaves. The protected Snowdon lily also grows here – this plant, which looks more like a daisy than a lily, only grows on

Llyn Ogwen, said to contain Excalibur, King Arthur's sword.

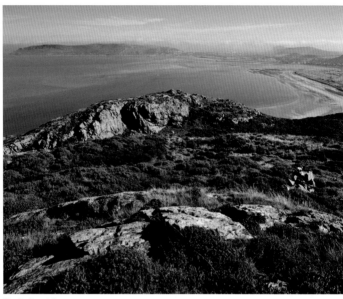

The Sychnant Pass.

Snowdon and the surrounding area. From the far end of Llyn Idwal an exhilarating but very steep path climbs through the rocky cleft known as the Devil's Kitchen (Twll Du) to Llyn y Cwn and on up to the boulder-strewn Glyder tops or the smoother-contoured Y Garn. On the lake's eastern side rise the Idwal Slabs, easy-angled rock faces often used by novice climbers 'learning the ropes'.

Penrhyn Castle

Wriggling from the mountains' grasp, the A5 delivers motorists down the dramatic Nant Ffrancon Valley to Bethesda, named after one of the town's many slate workers' chapels. It might as readily have been 'Jerusalem' or 'Siloam'. Southwest of the town, hemming it in, are the vast Penrhyn Slate Quarries that once employed 2000 men and are reckoned to be the deepest in the world. Still in operation today but with a workforce around

200, they were begun in Elizabethan times, and greatly expanded on the initiative of Thomas Pennant from Liverpool. Today it is also home to **Zip World's Velocity** (www.zipworld. co.uk; booking advisable; charge) allegedly the fastest zip line in the world and the longest in Europe. A short drive beyond the A55 towards Bangor will locate the National Trust's **Penrhyn Castle** ⑫ (www.national trust.org.uk/visit/wales/penrhyn-castle-and-garden; charge), Pennant's ostentatious, neo-Norman seat, set amidst glorious and extensive grounds. As well as fine interior craftsmanship – including a vast slate bed made for Queen Victoria – there are restored kitchens and a railway museum.

Sychnant Pass

Turn right onto the A55 coastal Expressway to Abergwyngregyn, which flanks the Carneddau foothills with wonderful views over to Anglesey and

Conwy Bay. Note that a lane southeast from Abergwyngregyn leads to a Forestry Commission car park near Bont Newydd, start of a popular and easy 3-mile (5km) round walk to view Aber Falls. The larger cascade – Rhaedr Fawr – plunges 170ft (52m) into the boulder-choked Afon Aber.

On the A55 beyond Llanfairfechan, watch for the turn-off to Penmaenmawr, a seaside town. From here, take the road towards Dwygyfylchi and to Sychnant Pass between Conwy and Bangor. There are walks in both directions from the pass, with marvellous views of Puffin Island and the Vale of Conwy.

Eating Out

RUTHIN
The Sugar Plum Tea Room
The Old Station, Rhewl;
www.sugarplumtearoom.co.uk.
Just north of Ruthin on the A525 Denbigh Road in the village of Rhewl, this colourful, fully-licenced, tea room forms part of a family interiors business. It's the perfect place to stop for breakfast, coffee, light lunch or afternoon tea. The full luxury tea experience (from 2pm) is expensive but you do get a huge range of home-made goodies and some prosecco. £

LLANDUDNO
The Cottage Loaf
147 Mostyn Street; http://the-cottageloaf.co.uk.
This gastropub offers a traditional pub and dining experience, with fine local ales complementing a homemade menu. There's a sheltered patio and relaxing garden room – an ideal setting for tucking into the likes of roasted aubergine and lentil dahl or a gourmet steak burger. ££

Osborne's Café
17 North Parade; www.osbornehouse.co.uk; closed Sun & Mon.
Café is hardly the word to describe this opulent hotel restaurant, which offers Michelin-recommended food at very reasonable prices. There are set menus available, with mains such as local lamb shank. Osborne's also serve an afternoon tea, complete with smoked salmon, *bara brith* and scones. ££

CONWY
Erskine Arms
Rose Hill Street;
www.erskinearms.co.uk.
Located not far from the castle, the Erskine Arms is a traditional Georgian coaching inn, which serves wholesome dishes using local produce, including Welsh beef and lamb. Lighter meals are available, too, including traditional Welsh rarebit and a range of sandwiches and paninis. ££

LLANRWST
Tu Hwnt I'r Bont
Near Inigo Jones Bridge;
www.tuhwntirbont.co.uk.
This extraordinary fifteenth-century cottage is perched beside the river at Llanrwst and belongs to the National Trust. It makes a picturesque place to stop for a sandwich or a ploughman's lunch. Their Traditional Bara Brith ('speckled bread') is a must-try. £

BETWS-Y-COED
Hangin' Pizzeria
Betws-y-Coed train station;
www.hanginpizzeria.co.uk.
Worthy cause aside – a percentage of the profits go to the Great Ape Conservation, hence the name – these are seriously good pizzas (Welsh rarebit and mozzarella, plus excellent vegan options), and if the weather's playing ball, you can enjoy them on the benches outside. £

The old lighthouse on Llanddwyn Island.

TOUR 2
A Tour of Anglesey

This 93-mile (150km) full-day tour takes you through the pastoral landscapes of Anglesey, which present a striking contrast to the more rugged mainland.

Anglesey – Ynys Môn to the Welsh – is Britain's largest offshore island. It is joined to the mainland by two engineering marvels which span the treacherous Menai Strait: Thomas Telford's elegant suspension bridge and George Stephenson's Britannia Bridge.

Heathland, pasture and fen spread gently westwards, punctuated by wind-honed copses and villages of single-storey, pebble-dashed houses crouched against the winter winds that sweep up through St George's Channel. The island's unique character distinguishes it from the rest of Snowdonia yet you are constantly reminded of its proximity by the glorious panorama of mountains spread along the eastern horizon. Much of Anglesey's shoreline enjoys Heritage Coast or AONB (Area of Outstanding

Highlights
- Llanfair Pwllgwyngyll
- Newborough Warren
- Barclodiad y Gawres
- Holy Island
- Moelfre
- Llangefni
- Beaumaris

Natural Beauty) status, a wonderful succession of dunes and river estuaries, islands, coves and bird-haunted sea cliffs; there are glorious sandy bays too.

Anglesey's long history has woven a rich tapestry of fascinating sites, from Neolithic times through the Industrial Revolution to the twenty-first century. In the fishing villages and around

Conwy suspension bridge.

the coast there are many associations with shipwrecks and smuggling, while inland a profusion of wildlife co-exists with a rural economy that until the 19th century derived much of its power from windmills, the stumps of which still dot the countryside.

The A4080 and A5025 roads virtually encircle the island, with the A5 striking more directly northwest to its terminus at Holyhead. However, you get more intimate glimpses of coast and interior if you explore country lanes along the way – this is not a place to be rushed. A visit to Oriel Ynys Môn on the outskirts of Llangefni will give you insights into the island's distinctive culture, history and environment.

The Bryn Celli Ddu burial mound.

The Britannia Bridge

To start the tour, follow the A5122 from Bangor and join the A55 over Stephenson's **Britannia Bridge** (Pont Britannia) ❶, which was built in 1850 to carry two railway tracks, each enclosed in an iron tube. A fire in 1970 so damaged the tubes that the bridge was closed while new arches were installed and a new road deck added on top.

Turn left onto the A4080 and note on the right the 100ft (30m) Marquess of Anglesey's Column. It commemorates the Marquess's heroic wounding at the Battle of Waterloo, when he exclaimed to the Duke of Wellington: 'By god sir, I've lost my leg!', to which the Duke replied: 'By god, so you have!'

Plas Newydd

Watch for the A4080's left turn at **Llanfairpwllgwyngyllgogerychwyrndrobwllllantysiliogogogoch** ❷ ('St Mary's Church in the hollow of the white hazel near the rapid whirlpool and the church of St Tysilio close to the red cave'). This tongue-twisting place name – generally shortened to the more manageable Llanfair PG or Llanfair Pwllgwyngyll – was probably invented in the nineteenth century by a local tradesman who was keen to attract tourists. It is certainly Britain's longest place name, with a railway

Neolithic site

Anglesey is full of Neolithic sites, and Bryn Celli Ddu, on the A4080, is one of the most important. Once a place of worship, it looks rather like a brooding hump in the landscape. Stones surround a polygonal stone burial chamber in which were found arrowheads, mussel shells, bones and a stone bead. The site can be visited at any time.

The country house and gardens of Plas Newydd.

station nameplate of national repute. A short detour off the A4080, towards the village of Llanddaniel Fab, would take you to one of Anglesey's most important Neolithic sites, Bryn Celli Ddu, a well-preserved chambered tomb (see page 29).

In 1.5 miles (2.5km) the road passes the National Trust's **Plas Newydd** ❸ (www.nationaltrust.org.uk/visit/wales/plas-newydd-house-and-garden; charge). This magnificent eighteenth-century neo-Gothic mansion is set in sloping parkland overlooking the

Whistler as Romeo

English artist Rex Whistler (1905–44) was noted for his extravagant murals and trompe l'œil paintings. His wall painting at Plas Newydd is believed to contain references to his love for the daughter of the house, Lady Caroline. Kids will enjoy trying to spot the artist in this extravagant work – he's in one corner depicted as Romeo, with Lady Caroline as Juliet, in the famous balcony scene. However, she didn't marry the lovelorn Whistler but somebody else. Whistler was killed in Normandy towards the end of World War II by a mortar bomb.

Menai Strait and the Snowdonia mountains. It was the home of the first Marquess of Anglesey, who commanded the cavalry at Waterloo, but was redesigned in later years. A museum is dedicated to the Marquess, who lost his leg in the battle. Its interior pièce de résistance is an extraordinary 58ft (18m) -wide trompe l'oeil mural painted in 1937 by Rex Whistler. Taking up a whole wall, it is an extravagant scene, encompassing the Snowdonia mountains and Portmeirion. The gardens are well worth exploring, with fine displays of rhododendrons in the spring.

From Plas Newydd, return to the A4080 and through the village of Brynsiencyn, which stands surrounded by an ancient landscape of prehistoric dolmens and burial mounds.

Newborough Warren

The A4080 continues to Newborough at the island's southwest tip. Since Elizabeth I's reign, marram grass has been planted to stabilise the shifting dunes here in **Newborough Warren** ❹. Before 1930, when afforestation began, the grass was woven into mats and brushes while the warren's rabbit population provided valuable protein for the local diet. A forestry toll road runs down to Llanddwyn Bay's 4-mile (6.5km) -long beach, and there are walks in the 2,000-acre (800-hectare) Newborough Forest. The area has been designated a National Nature Reserve and is extremely rich in wildlife. Plants include orchids and butterworts, skylarks can often be heard, and there is a multitude of

Parys mountain.

Druids' last stand

The Druids were Celtic religious leaders who had a powerful base on Anglesey. They are said to have preached immortality through rebirth and to occasionally have made human sacrifices. Caesar wrote of them as a 'privileged class', and they provided strong opposition to the Roman forces. The Romans gradually pushed them out of mainland Wales, until they were isolated on Anglesey and finally massacred around AD 61.

invertebrates, including the medicinal leech. In winter, the mudflats become home to a variety of birds including pintail, wigeon and redshank. Near Newborough Warren is a finger of land known as Llanddwyn Island, here there is a breeding population of cormorants. It is associated with St Dwynwen, a fifth-century saint who is the Welsh patron saint of lovers. Her feast day is 25 January.

For almost 30 years before his death in 1979 the wildlife artist Charles Tunnicliffe lived at Malltraeth, recording the island's landscapes and especially its birds. His work is represented in Oriel Ynys Môn at Llangefni.

Aberffraw to Holy Island

Immense sandhills separate **Aberffraw's** beach from road and village as the route proceeds along the A4080. Here was an ancient seat of the powerful Princes of Gwynedd and their main Court (Llys) up to the thirteenth century. However, nothing remains of the original timber buildings.

An alternative A4080 loop route a little further north, leads to Rhosneigr (from Rhos y Neidr, 'Moor of the Adder'), perched on a little rocky promontory at the mouth of the Afon Crigyll. Its demure whitewashed cottages belie a darker past when a gang of wreckers lured ships onto this rugged shore. They were finally caught and hanged at Beaumaris in 1741 and later became the subject of a local ballad.

Newborough Warrens.

Lighthouse on South Stack.

If you're interested in Anglesey's Neolithic past, then stop at Llanfaelog, at the Wayside Stores to visit **Barclodiad y Gawres** ❺ (www.cadw. gov.wales/visit/places-to-visit/barclodiad-y-gawres-burial-chamber; free). This is possibly the most important Neolithic site in Wales, and sits a mile (1.6km) away, northwest of Aberffraw on the Anglesey Coastal Path. It is reached by a locked gate; staff at the stores have a key and can accompany you. Barclodiad y Gawres, managed by Cadw (the Welsh Assembly's historic environment division), is a fine example of a passage grave. It was built around 3000 BC and features stones that have been decorated with spirals and swirls.

Fork left just under half a mile (500m) northeast of Llanfaelog, joining the A5 just before Bryngwran for Holyhead. At Caergeiliog, plane-spotters can take the lane south to the railway bridge at Llanfair-yn-Neubwll, or further to Carnau, there to watch the comings and goings at RAF Valley with its training school for jet pilots and air-sea rescue station.

Holy Island

A detour out to **Holy Island** (Ynys Gybi) is recommended. This small island just off Anglesey (they're connected by a bridge) got its name as it was settled in the sixth century by a monk, St Cybi, a cousin of St David. The B4545 to Treaddur Bay gives way to tortuous lanes over to **South Stack** ❻, a rocky islet reached by pedestrian bridge at the bottom of 350 steps. Over 4000 pairs of seabirds, including puffins, guillemots, razorbills and fulmars, breed in this RSPB reserve (www.rspb.org.uk) each spring and early summer, observable from the Ellin's Tower Visitor Centre (free). You may also spot ravens and peregrines, while the heathland is important for the chough. Choughs are the rarest type of crow in the UK, and South Stack has several breeding pairs.

The nearby Gogarth Bay sea cliffs are a popular rock-climbing venue and there are also clifftop walks to North Stack. At 722ft (220m), **Holyhead Mountain** is Anglesey's highest ground by far, with views to match. Hut circles and the large Caer y Twr, an Iron Age

Parys Mountain.

hillfort, indicate mankind's occupation of this exposed peninsula spanning many centuries.

Holyhead

Holyhead ❼ (Caergybi) is Anglesey's largest town and an important sea port for services to Dublin. The arrival of Telford's road from London in 1821, marked by a triumphal Doric arch, and the railway shortly afterwards, transformed the harbour's fortunes. A huge breakwater almost 2 miles (3km) long was built (it took 30 years) to protect the anchorage's 700 acres (280 hectares) from northwesterly gales. In the centre of the town is **St Cybi's church**, founded by the saint in an abandoned Roman fortress. The church pews have pagan Green Men carved on the ends, and there are Pre-Raphaelite stained-glass windows by William Morris and Edward Burne-Jones.

North from Holyhead, lanes branch out from the A5025 towards the shore of Holyhead Bay where coves and low cliffs alternate towards Carmel Head. Offshore lie the Skerries and West Mouse islands, hazards in the days of sail when anxious Liverpool shipowners awaited news of their vessels.

North Coast

Anglesey's north coast is closely shadowed by roads, but there is a fine stretch of coastal footpath too, especially between Cemaes and Amlwch. Car parks at both ends of Cemlyn Bay's great shingle bank and lagoon allow access for walking and for viewing seabirds. Wales' only nuclear power station, the **Wylfa Power Station**, can be seen west of Cemlyn Bay. The present station is being decommissioned before a new plant is due to be built. Before Amlwch's ascendancy in the late eighteenth century, Cemaes and Porthlechog (Bull's Bay) were centres for fishing, coastal trade and smuggling. **Amlwch** itself became a boom town when top-grade copper ore was discovered in nearby Parys Mountain during 1768. The ore was dug in open-cast workings and within 30 years the population had exploded to 6000. Competition from cheaper American and African copper eventually ended the UK boom. The 'moonscape' of Parys Mountain, along with Llyn Alaw, Anglesey's largest lake, lies just to the south.

Moelfre

Extensive sands characterise Anglesey's sheltered eastern coast, particularly bordering Dulas, Lligwy and Red Wharf bays; in between, however, treacherous rocks have caused many a shipwreck. It was north of Moelfre in October 1859 that the steam clipper *Royal Charter*, inward bound from the Australian goldfields, foundered in huge seas with the loss of over 450 lives and an estimated £370,000 of prospectors' gold. Visit **Moelfre ❽** where its **Seawatch Centre** (tel: 01248 410300; free), run by the Royal National Lifeboat Institution, gives an insight into the maritime heritage of the area. Not far from Moelfre (signposted from the roundabout on the A5025 southwest of the village) is Lligwy, site of **Din Lligwy**, the remains of a first-century farmstead probably settled during the Roman occupation. One of the most

impressive ancient sites in Britain, it may have been the home of a Celtic chieftain; some buildings still possess substantial walls with doorposts and traces of drainage systems across the floor. Nearby is **Lligwy burial chamber** (cadw.gov.wales/visit/places-to-visit/lligwy-burial-chamber; free), a late Neolithic tomb that contained the remains of around 30 individuals. The tomb would originally have been covered with earth. In a field is the ruined chapel **Capel Lligwy**, which dates back to the twelfth century. For unrivalled panoramic views, climb to the little 584ft (178m) summit of Mynydd Bodafon, reached up a lane off the A5025.

Llangefni

Half a mile (0.8km) south of the Moelfre roundabout, turn right onto the B5110. The administrative capital of Anglesey and its principal market town, **Llangefni ❾** epitomises the island's rural Welsh heart. Although the traditional cattle market has moved out of the town centre, The Square, near the Bull Hotel, remains a constantly bustling focal point. On the town's outskirts along the B5111 to the north stands **Oriel Ynys Môn** (www.orielmon.org/en-gb; free), which houses an excellent permanent exhibition featuring Anglesey's history,

---

A puffin cruise

Seacoast Safaris (www.seacoast safaris.co.uk) run 80-minute boat trips from Beaumaris Pier around Puffin Island, also known as Seiriol's Island after the small monastic community established here by St Seiriol. The island provides a home to seabirds such as puffins and razorbills. You may also spot some seals on the trip.

Uninhabited Puffin Island is the site of a protected seabird colony.

Beaumaris Gaol.

holes' and arrow slits. The castle last saw action in 1646, during the English Civil War. Opposite stands the seventeenth-century **Courthouse** (tel: 01248 810921; charge), which was last used as a court in 1971. Visitors can stand in the dock, and find out about past trials on Anglesey.

Behind the Parish Church to the west you will find the nineteenth-century **Gaol** (www.visitanglesey. co.uk/en/things-to-do/activities/ beaumaris-gaol; charge; joint tickets available). This Victorian structure, built by the man who designed the Hansom cab, provides a grim reminder of prison life in earlier times. The gaol contains an original tread wheel (used as punishment), and a gibbet. Visitors can see the cells, including the condemned cell, and even handle chains that were used to shackle the unfortunate prisoners.

Penmon Priory

To visit **Penmon Priory** ruins and St Seiriol's Well, take the B5109 north and follow signs along the narrow

Penmon Church.

culture and environment. There are artefacts from the wrecked *Royal Charter*, and Neolithic items ranging from flints to a gold ring. Part of the space is devoted to the work of the wildlife artist Charles Tunnicliffe, and there is also a Kyffin Williams gallery featuring the eponymous artist's work.

Beaumaris

Follow the B5109 via Pentraeth to **Beaumaris** ⑩ (from 'beau maris', Norman-French for 'beautiful marsh'). Last in Edward I's chain of coastal fortresses against the Welsh, **Beaumaris Castle** (Castle Street; www.cadw.gov.wales; charge) dates back to 1295 and is Britain's most technically perfect medieval castle, with concentric rings of defensive walls inside a deep moat; there was even a jetty that enabled provisioning to take place from the sea. It was designed by Edward 1's architect Master James of St George. It was certainly intended to repel all attackers, with inner walls up to 16ft (4.8m) thick, as well as 'murder access lanes. The original priory, founded here and on neighbouring Priestholm (Puffin Island) in the sixth century by the hermit St Seiriol, was burnt down by the Danes. The present Penmon Church, containing some splendid Norman features, dates from the twelfth century, the associated monastic buildings from the thirteenth to the sixteenth centuries. East of the priory, a massive dovecote was built around 1600 to house up to 1000 pigeons destined for the table of local landowner Sir Richard Bulkeley. It is near St Seiriol's Well, which was once said to have had healing properties.

The A545 leads along the shoreline of the Menai Strait to Menai Bridge where **Thomas Telford's Suspension Bridge** is crossed.

The high street in Beaumaris, a major yachting centre.

Eating Out

ABERFFRAW
The Crown
Bodorgan Square; www.thecrown aberffraw.co.uk.
A super local pub with a surprisingly good menu and a very friendly welcome. Keen to support local food producers and breweries; expect some great home cooking such as steak and ale pie and local lamb shank, while the Sunday roast goes down a treat here. ££

RHOSCOLYN, HOLY ISLAND
The White Eagle
Rhoscolyn; www.white-eagle.co.uk
You get sea views from this popular pub which offers old favourites such as fish and chips, as well as steaks, Welsh lamb, plus good vegetarian options. Desserts include a satisfying sticky-toffee pudding. There's a fantastic beer garden too. ££

NR HOLYHEAD
The Lobster Pot
Church Bay, Rhydwyn; www.

thelobsterpot.uk; closed Sun & Mon.
A former traditional longhouse, this restaurant has dark beams and is simply furnished, allowing the food to take centre stage. As the name suggests, it specialises in local seafood; the menu features oysters, lobsters and crabs. Some meat dishes and vegetarian options are available and are less expensive. There are also some wickedly decadent deserts. £££

BEAUMARIS
The Bull
Castle Street; www.inncollection group.com/bulls-head-inn.
This slick, popular inn also has a more informal restaurant called *Coach*. Try tomato gazpacho for starters, followed by whole-dressed Welsh crab; desserts include melting chocolate sphere, or tuck into a selection of delicious Welsh cheese. There's a kid-friendly menu and daily specials. Afterwards, unwind with a drink at their bar. ££

BARDS AND LEGENDS

The Welsh tradition of story-telling is a strong one,
continuing down through generations from its origins
in the Dark Ages to the modern period.

Monsters and dragons

The most important collection of
medieval tales – the four branches of
the Mabinogion – is contained in two
texts from around the mid-fourteenth
century: the White Book of Rhydderch
and the Red Book of Hergest. Although
these tales were written down around
the thirteenth century, they are
considered to be of much earlier origin.
They weren't translated into English
until the nineteenth century when their

translator, Lady Charlotte Guest, gave
them their collective title which means
'Tales of Youth'. Amongst the characters
featured is King Arthur, together with
his knights. Monsters and dragons also
feature widely in North Wales' folklore.
The red dragon, now on the Welsh
national flag, appears in the Mabinogion
and also a later legend in which two
dragons – one red, one white – sleep
beneath Dinys Emrys in Snowdonia:
the red dragon symbolised the Celts; the
white, the Saxons. The dragons fought

Druidic ceremony during National Eisteddfod.

an eye with the effort, which shed tears to form Pwll Llygad yr Ych (Pool of the Ox's Eye). Struggling up into Cwm Dyli, past Llyn Llydaw, the exhausted team finally released the *afanc* into the deep waters of Llyn Ffynnon Las (Lake of the Blue Fountain), now called Glaslyn. And there he dwells to this day.

The Eisteddfod

The medieval Welsh story-teller (*y cyfarwydd* – the learned one), like the poet, enjoyed a high social status as court entertainer. He needed a powerful memory and expert narrative techniques to re-create tales and folklore at each performance. The Eisteddfod ('gathering') dates back to meetings between Celtic bards, when they would compete for positions in court and in wealthy households. The first recorded bardic contest was that of 1176, convened at Cardigan castle by Rhys ap Gruffydd. It was proclaimed a year and a day in advance (a custom still observed) to ensure high standards; miniature silver chains were presented as prizes for poetry and music. In the nineteenth century the tradition, which had begun to die out, was revived with an internationally significant Eisteddfod held in Carmarthen. In 1880 the National Eisteddfod of Wales (tickets tel: 0845 4090 800; www.eisteddfod.org.uk) was formed to stage an annual festival to promote high cultural standards, and help to safeguard the Welsh language. One of Europe's largest arts and music festivals, the Eisteddfod is held alternately in North and South Wales during the first week of August and is a traditional neo-druidic ceremony, occurring within a specially laid-out Gorsedd Circle of Stones to the accompaniment of harp music. The 2024 festival is to be held in Pontypridd and in 2025 it will be in Wrexham.

and the red was the victor. Henry Tudor, on his way to Bosworth, flew a flag emblazoned with a dragon.

Another legend features the *afanc* of Glaslyn, whose supernatural powers were upsetting people in the Vale of Conwy, causing disastrous floods, ruining crops and drowning livestock. It lived in a Beaver Pool near Betws-y-coed. When elders decided to remove it to some other distant lake, they forged strong iron chains and got two mighty oxen ready. A damsel lured the *afanc* from its underwater lair (it evidently had a predilection for beautiful maidens), whereupon it was tethered to the oxen and dragged through the parish of Dolwyddelan. Over the shoulder between Moel Siabod and Cribau – Bwlch Rhiw-yr-Ychain (Pass of the Oxen's Slope) – they went, one ox losing

View of the Snowdon range from Porthmadog.

TOUR 3
Beddgelert and Porthmadog

At 81 miles (130km) this tour takes you to some of the best-known spots in Snowdonia, passing sights of great scenic beauty, industrial heritage and rich history.

Throughout Snowdonia one finds echoes of those intrepid Victorians who flocked to the region in a search for scenery that embodied notions of the romantic and picturesque. The Napoleonic Wars in Europe meant that they were unable to embark on the Grand Tour, which took them over the dramatic mountains of the Alps to great cities such as Florence and Rome. And so, seeking equivalent drama at home, they went to the Highlands of Scotland, the Lake District and North Wales, making resorts out of sleepy hamlets and establishing a trend for enjoying the great outdoors. Angling, walking, climbing, sketching or simply admiring the scenery all drew visitors to this part of Wales, among them William Wordsworth, Sir Walter Scott

Highlights
- Beddgelert
- Porthmadog
- Ffestiniog Railway
- Blaenau Ffestiniog and Slate Caverns
- Dolwyddelan Castle
- Ty Mawr Wybrnant

and the painter J.M.W. Turner. This popularisation spurred the development of such places as Betws-y-coed, Capel Curig, Beddgelert and Dolwyddelan.

The less well-off local population still had to work for a living, often in arduous conditions. Copper mining, agriculture and fishing continued to employ labour as they had for

The best choirs compete at the National Eisteddfod.

Male voice choirs

Choral music came to Wales with non-conformity – and chapels put great emphasis on hymn singing. But it was industrialisation that brought male voice choirs, which in Victorian times could be 150 strong. The distinctive sound is less frequently heard today, but there are still choirs in North Wales and visitors are usually welcome to attend rehearsals. Just ask the local tourist office for details.

41

TOUR 3 LLYN GWYNANT

centuries, but it was the building trade's insatiable appetite for roofing slate that brought about the greatest changes and opportunities. The hills around Blaenau Ffestiniog and many other locations were devastated by quarrying, their slate transported by narrow-gauge railway to quaysides on the coast, such as those at Porthmadog.

Betws-y-coed

This tour starts in **Betws-y-coed** ❶ where the A5 climbs past Swallow Falls to reach the straggling village of Capel Curig (see page 24). Take the A4086 past Plas y Brenin, Wales's National Mountain Sports Centre, which runs courses in an enormous variety of outdoor disciplines, and

A wood craft shop in Beddgelert.

enjoys a classic view of Snowdon seen across the waters of Llynnau Mymbyr. The Nantygwryd valley forms a broad trench between Moel Siabod (2861ft/872m) and the Glyder range, whose rugged slopes fill northern views right along to the Pen y Gwryd junction. Up to the right lies Pen-y-Pass, starting point for two popular paths up Snowdon and, beyond, the Llanberis Pass (see page 56).

Llyn Gwynant

Keep straight on along the A498 and in a mile (1.6km) or so there are lay-bys from which to admire the Snowdon massif from the east. Cwm Dyli, a deep U-shaped hollow containing hydro-electric pipelines, was scoured out by an Ice Age glacier which then turned abruptly southwest to form the valley Nantgwynant. The road coils narrowly downhill to beautiful, shingle-beached **Llyn Gwynant**. At its southern end hills encroach, forming a glen connecting with Llyn Dinas. Strangely reminiscent of a Chinese landscape painting, this area was chosen in 1958 as a location for filming *Inn of the Sixth Happiness*. Unseen up to the left, the Moelwyn hills cradle myriad small lakes, but they are quite remote and only accessible on foot.

The story of Gelert

Gelert was Prince Llewellyn's dog. Legend has it that the prince left the dog to guard his little son, but when he returned he discovered the bed empty and covered in blood – with the child missing. Llewellyn assumed Gelert had killed the little boy and he murdered the faithful dog – only to discover the child lying safe nearby, beside the body of a dead wolf which Gelert had bravely killed. However, it's thought that an enterprising publican made up the tale to attract visitors in the eighteenth century. It seemed to work.

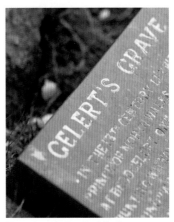

The grave can be found by following a riverside footpath.

Sygun Copper Mine

Yr Aran (2451ft/747m) rears a shapely head to the north and the road reaches **Sygun Copper Mine ❷** (www.sygun coppermine.co.uk; charge). Begun around 1830 but never a commercial success owing to the low-grade ore, Sygun mine was abandoned in 1903. Extensively restored since then, you can take a self-guided audio tour of the tunnels and chambers, learn about the lives of the miners who worked here and see veins of copper ore. The mine is characterised by its green stalactites and stalagmites. There's also a small museum, containing an array of oddities like dinosaur eggs, Stone Age coins and a mammoth tooth.

Beddgelert

There are scenic paths over to Cwm Bychan and the Pass of Aberglaslyn,

Beddgelert.

while an unclassified mountain road with picnic areas runs from Pont Bethania through Nantmor. However, the main road itself goes through **Beddgelert** ❸, which is surely the prettiest village in North Wales. Its buildings are clustered around the confluence of the Glaslyn and Colwyn rivers beneath the dominant presence of Moel Hebog (2569ft/783m). Alfred Bestall, who created the comic character Rupert Bear for the *Daily Express* newspaper, spent schoolboy holidays here and later purchased a house in the village called Penlan; many of the scenes pictured in the comic strip were inspired by the scenery at Beddgelert. Bestall died in 1986.

Beddgelert has been immortalised by the apocryphal legend of Gelert,

Llewellyn the Great's faithful hound – *bedd* means grave in Welsh. **Gelert's Grave** can be seen just to the south of the village, under a tree in a meadow by the Afon Glaslyn. However, it's more likely that the grave referred to is not that of the dog, but that of Celert, a sixth-century Celtic saint. St Mary's Church in the village has sixth-century origins. The religious community eventually established an Augustinian priory here, but it was destroyed by fire in the thirteenth century. Although restored, it then suffered after the Dissolution of the monasteries in Henry VIII's reign, and today the church is all that is left.

Beddgelert, which boasts a great ice-cream shop, makes an excellent base for exploring Snowdonia and is a starting point for walks of all kinds,

Porthmadog's marina.

from easy rambles to mountain hikes. You can also hire bikes in the village and explore the surrounding forest tracks. Beddgelert is a stop on the marvellous Welsh Highland Railway, a restored steam railway that runs from Caernarfon (see page 51).

Tremadog

Having left Beddgelert, keep right at the Pass of Aberglaslyn, still on the A498. The route goes through woods with tantalising views of Tremadog

Tremadog Bay.

Bay, then clings to the western edge of reclaimed marshland on the Afon Glaslyn's flood plain, before reaching Tremadog, best known for its roadside rock-climbing crags and the nearby café. T.E. Lawrence (Lawrence of Arabia) was born in the village which was developed as a staging post in the early nineteenth century by William Madocks (1773–1828), Member of Parliament for Boston, Lincolnshire. It formed part of his ambitious, though ultimately unsuccessful, scheme to establish a new mail route to Ireland using Porth Dinllaen on the north coast of the Lleyn Peninsula (see page 62). **Tremadog** was a carefully planned settlement, and had one of the first woollen mills in Wales. The town's chapel is unusual, built in the style of a Greek temple, while St Mary's Church was built in the nineteenth century in neo-Gothic style.

Porthmadog

Turn left onto the A487 and into **Porthmadog ❹**. These days Porthmadog is a bustling holiday centre for outdoor activities, and a real hub for steam railway fans, but in times past its prosperity was dependent

The Ffestiniog train.

on the slate industry. From its quaysides, ships loaded with Ffestiniog slate, brought down by narrow-gauge railway from the great quarries around Blaenau Ffestiniog, set sail for destinations worldwide. The small but interesting **Porthmadog Maritime Museum** (www.portmm.org; charge), located in the last remaining slate shed on the harbour, charts the seafaring history of the town.

Porthmadog itself was designed by William Madocks. A path from the harbour leads along to neighbouring Borth-y-Gest, another erstwhile slate port with a curving quay backed by cottages.

The world-renowned narrow-gauge, steam **Ffestiniog Railway** (www.festrail.co.uk) began life in 1832, conveying industrial slate from the great Ffestiniog quarries to Porthmadog quay. It ceased operating in 1946, but was enthusiastically rescued from oblivion in 1954, and since then has enjoyed burgeoning popularity. The full 13.5-mile (22km) journey takes an hour each way and provides spectacular views from the carriage windows, especially outside the season of full tree foliage. It goes from sea level at Porthmadog and climbs 700ft (213m) into the mountains. Connections with the

Purple Moose Brewery logo.

A local brew

If you'd like to pick up some traditionally brewed local beers, then call in to the Purple Moose Brewery shop in Porthmadog (27 High Street; www.purplemoose.co.uk), which stocks their entire range. Better still head to the Purple Moose-owned Australia pub, just up the road at no.31, where you can also tuck into one of their delicious ale-infused pies.

The Bala Lake Railway.

Great Welsh railways

Wales is a great destination for anyone who loves scenic railway journeys. The country industrialised extremely early and rail links were built to carry goods quickly to ports and markets. When the industries declined, so did the railways. However, enthusiastic volunteers have restored many of these routes into tourist lines, frequently using vintage steam locomotives. As well as the well-known Ffestiniog and Welsh Highland railways, there is the Bala Lake Railway (www.bala-lake-railway.co.uk) which runs for 9 miles/14km along Lake Bala from Llanuwchllyn, and the Llanberis Lake Railway (www.lake-railway.co.uk), a narrow-gauge steam railway from Gilfach Ddu to Lake Padarn and back. To the east of the Snowdonia National Park is the Llangollen Railway (www.llangollen-railway.co.uk), which runs 10 miles (16km) from Llangollen to Corwen, while in the west is the coastal Fairbourne to Barmouth steam railway (www.fairbournerailway.com).

Conwy Valley Line (www.conwyvalleyrailway.co.uk) at Blaenau Ffestiniog open up numerous travel permutations, as the 27-mile (43km) line goes to Betws-y-coed and then Llandudno. At Porthmadog, the Ffestiniog Railway connects with the **Welsh Highland Railway** (www.festrail.co.uk). This runs for 25 miles (40km) to Caernarfon. The route goes by the brooding presence of Snowdon, then into Beddgelert before its terminus at Caernarfon, and the majority of trains are steam hauled.

Maentwrog

Cheek by jowl with the railway, the road crosses the mile-long (1.6km) embankment across the Glaslyn estuary known as **The Cob**, a famous Madocks creation behind which some 7000 acres (2800 hectares) were reclaimed from the sea. If visibility is good, there are stunning mountain views over the estuary. The shapeliest cone is Cnicht (2261ft/689m), the so-called 'Welsh Matterhorn'. In about a mile (1.6km), Minffordd is reached where the Ffestiniog and main Cambrian Coast Line between Pwllheli and Aberystwyth intersect, each with a station allowing interchange. Beyond Penrhyndeudraeth (headquarters of the Snowdonia National Park) the A487 follows the Afon Dwyryd to Tan-y-bwlch in the lovely Vale of Ffestiniog. Once over the river it joins the A496 near the pretty village of **Maentwrog**, named after a large stone in the churchyard said to have been thrown there from the hills above by the giant Twrog. The novelist Thomas Love Peacock, a friend of the poet Shelley, spent much time here, eventually marrying the local rector's daughter. Another literary association involves the great English poet Gerard Manley Hopkins who found inspiration for his work during a visit here. Follow the road, then bear north on the A470 to Blaenau Ffestiniog.

Blaenau Ffestiniog

When the National Park was designated in 1952, **Blaenau Ffestiniog ❺** and neighbouring Tanygrisiau were excluded: national park criteria were hardly met, it was argued, by an area of decaying slate tips, disused quarries and high local unemployment requiring an influx of alternative industries. It still rains for over 100 days each year in Blaenau Ffestiniog and by traditional yardsticks the surroundings remain bleak, yet this has become part of Blaenau's very appeal. The landscape of brooding grey slate possesses a sense of drama that you find in few places in the UK. Since the early days public perceptions have changed, particularly in regard to industrial archeology, and although the area has yet to be included in the National Park, in 2021, it became Wales' fourth UNESCO World Heritage Site. Tourism has certainly transformed Blaenau's fortunes. Witness, for example, the success of the **Llechwedd Slate Caverns** (www.llechwedd.co.uk), a highly educational and absorbing tourist attraction; great for children. There are three tours available year-round. The first is the Deep Mine Tour, in

Llechwedd Slate Caverns at Blaenau Ffestiniog.

Dolwyddelan Castle.

which you descend 500ft (152m) underground by cable railway, then follow a walk (one mile (1.6km) there and back and down 61 steps) through tunnels and caverns while listening to the digital retelling of the stories of men and boys working by candlelight. The second tour is the Quarry Explorer, a 90-minute guided journey around the quarry in a 4 x 4 truck. You drive to the summit of the quarry for fabulous views and down inside some of the huge craters. The final tour takes you into the slate workshops where you will see how the slates are split. Winter walking tours take you through a tunnel to the mine built in the 1840s. There's also a working pub, The Quarryman's Tavern.

Also within the quarry is **Zip World** (www.zipworld.co.uk; booking advisable), with its 4-person zip line Titan and underground bouncing nets, underground golf (the world's first), plus an adventure course on wires, rope bridges and more, down in the caverns.

At Tanygrisiau there are walks from the road-end up to Llyn Cwmorthin in a valley strewn with evocative relics from a bygone era of intensive slate working. A derelict chapel, ruined workers' cottages and abandoned slate sheds crouch beneath the brooding Moelwyn hills whose highest point – Moelwyn Mawr (2526ft/770m) – overlooks the Stwlan Dam.

Dolwyddelan Castle

The A470 climbs determinedly north to the Crimea Pass at 1263ft (385m) above sea level. Opinion is divided as to whether it was named after the mid-nineteenth-century war or a pub that once stood on the site of the present car park at the top. After locals repeatedly complained of rowdiness in 1910 the pub was demolished with true non-conformist vindictiveness.

Coming down off the pass facing vast views ahead, the road descends as a long dramatic sweep into the wooded valley of the Afon Lledr. It crosses the railway line, which has not long since emerged from a 2-mile (3km) -long tunnel, to reach **Dolwyddelan Castle** ❻ (www.cadw.gov.wales; free). Situated on a knoll on the southern slopes of Moel Siabod, a little way from the roadside car park along a good path, the castle stands over the route from the Conwy and Lledr valleys over to Dyffryn Maentwrog – broadly the way just followed. It was built by the Welsh in the late twelfth century, but its upper parts are a nineteenth-century reconstruction. Tradition has it that Llewellyn the Great was born here, though this is unlikely – it is more likely that he built it. In Dolwyddelan village, south of the main road, stands the delightful little sixteenth-century Old Church.

Ty Mawr Wybrant

With numerous twists and turns, the A470 drops eastwards towards the confluence of the Lledr and Machno rivers in woodland that becomes outstandingly beautiful when it dons its autumnal foliage. South from the A470, but only accessible on very narrow lanes, is the National Trust's **Ty Mawr Wybrant** ❼ (www.national trust.org.uk/visit/wales/ty-mawr-wybrnant; charge), a remote sixteenth-century farmhouse and birthplace of William Morgan who first translated the Bible into Welsh.

This was the result of an Act of Parliament in Elizabeth I's reign, which allowed translation into Welsh because so many people in Wales at that time did not understand English. In 1588 the first copies of the Welsh Bible were printed. The core Bible collection, which includes the prestigious item, is currently on display at Chirk Castle's library.

A minor road from Penmachno offers a pleasant return to Betws-y-coed. Penmachno village itself sits in an unspoilt valley and is well known for its weaving tradition.

Eating Out

BETWS-Y-COED

Alpine Coffee Shop
Station Approach;
www.alpinecoffeeshop.co.uk.
This welcoming café at Betws-y-coed railway station offers a varied menu featuring all-day breakfasts, home-made soups and Mediterranean boards, as well as mouthwatering afternoon teas. The coffee is excellent, too. There are plenty of vegetarian, vegan and gluten-free options and all dishes are palm-oil free. Dogs are welcome and invited to enjoy the local sausages. £

The Bridge Restaurant
Waterloo Hotel; www.waterloo-hotel.info.
This hotel bistro serves modern British dishes. Concentrating on local produce, choose from starters such as local-baked bread and olive platter, steaks and fish dishes, and a range of desserts. Vegetarian choices include a wild mushroom, spinach and tagliatelle dish. Wood-fired oven pizzas and grilled dishes also feature. ££

Ty Gwyn
By Waterloo Bridge;
www.tygwynhotel.co.uk.
This very popular inn serves a wide range of bar meals, and also has a restaurant. Dishes range from fresh fillet smoked cod or Welsh fillet steak to veggie yellow Thai curry. They also offer a cracking Sunday roast. Desserts might include honeycomb, chocolate and ginger cheesecake. ££

Caernarfon.

TOUR 4
Snowdon from Caernarfon

This 38-mile (62km) full day's tour will take you to Snowdon itself, the highest peak in Wales, before heading down to the coast and the ancient town of Caernarfon.

No visit to Snowdonia is complete without seeing Yr Wyddfa (Snowdon's Welsh name) at close quarters. Rising to 3560ft (1085m), it is the highest peak in England and Wales and one that offers itself generously to all who seek to explore its great crags and cwms (valleys).

There are six main tracks to the summit, while the less mobile may scale the heights by means of the famous Snowdon Mountain Railway. Needless to say, inexperienced hillwalkers should climb up only in good weather and should wear appropriate clothing.

Yr Wyddfa means 'tomb' or 'monument', a reference to the burial of the legendary Rhita Gawr, an ogre with a predilection for slaying

Highlights
- Caernarfon Castle
- Llanberis
- Snowdon Mountain Railway
- National Slate Museum
- Dolbadarn Castle
- The Pass of Llanberis

kings, who was himself killed at the summit by King Arthur. Botanist Thomas Johnson wrote the first account of an ascent in 1639, but it was Thomas Pennant's published tours that popularised the mountain in the late eighteenth century, and another Thomas – Telford – whose London to Holyhead road provided the accessibility. By the 1830s, guiding was already proving profitable, often using horses to convey visitors by the easier Llanberis Track. As early as 1854, on his famous tour of Wales, George Borrow found the track 'thronged with tourists as far as the eye could reach…' Accommodation and refreshments became available in wooden huts clustered around the huge summit cairn and operated by competing hotels in the valley. When the first train service began in 1896, a new era of summit building started, culminating in the demolition of the by-then squalid huts. The 1930s saw construction of a complex designed by Clough Williams-Ellis, creator of the Portmeirion Italianate village. Trains to the summit terminate at the Hafod Eryri visitor centre (see page 57).

Caernarfon

This drive starts down at sea level, in what is surely the most Welsh of towns; **Caernarfon ❶**. Caernarfon is a busy holiday town, market and administrative centre. Its old streets and alleyways, its Georgian houses

around The Square and its historic inns all exude flavours from a diverse past, and it is also the starting point for the vintage Welsh Highland Railway line (see page 46). Caernarfon has a rich history, as you'll find out at the **Segontium Roman Fort** (www.cadw. gov.wales; free), which sits to the southeast of the town centre on the A4085, where the foundations of a fort garrisoned by the twentieth Augustan legion can still be seen. The Romans had built the fort here to control the coast around Anglesey, which was where the Druids made their last stand against the invaders. The site was of great strategic importance as it also helped to protect against attacks from across the Irish Sea. Occupied from around AD 77 to AD 394, Segontium garrisoned around 1000 soldiers and was also an important administrative centre in Wales.

Caernarfon Castle

But above all Caernarfon is synonymous with the magnificent **Castle** (www.cadw.gov.wales; charge)

Caernarfon Castle.

The grassy interior of Caernarfon Castle.

This enormous castle was built by Edward I and joined part of his network of fortifications in Wales; the intention was to create a royal residence and seat of administrative power. It overlooks the Menai Strait and was of great symbolic significance:

it and the new surrounding town effectively erasing all visible signs of Welshness and embodying Edward I 's imperial dreams. Having ended the power of the native Welsh princes, the king even ensured that his son (later Edward II) was born at Caernarfon, and then conferred on him the title of Prince of Wales.

Although begun, along with Conwy Castle, in 1283, it was to be 43 years before the building was complete. Twice unsuccessfully besieged by Owain Glyndwr, fought over during the Civil Wars and captured by Parliamentary forces in 1646, the castle was finally condemned for demolition in 1660. Happily the exterior walls and three towers remain intact and are hugely impressive, though most of the interior has been lawned. The present Prince of Wales was invested here on 1 July 1969, an event which caused some local controversy which was perhaps not surprising given

Looking down on Caernarfon from the vantage point of the castle.

the castle's history. Housed in two towers of the castle is the fascinating **Regimental Museum** (www.rwf museum.org.uk; free with castle ticket) of the Royal Welch Fusiliers (they still use the ancient spelling of their name). The oldest regiment in Wales, their mascot is a goat.

Much of the town's present countenance dates from the nineteenth century, when it became the location of a thriving slate port. Victoria Dock is home to **Galeri Caernarfon** (www.galericaernarfon.com) a striking arts venue, whose stylish exterior reflects the area's industrial heritage. It has a 400-seat theatre, a cinema and a gallery, as well as a café. Galeri is at the centre of the on-going development of the Caernarfon waterside to create

Castles in Wales

William the Conqueror was the first to build castles in Wales, using them to impose his authority on the area. Most Norman castles are in the south and along the English/Welsh border. In the thirteenth century, Welsh princes began to build their own castles, which were smaller than Norman structures and sited on craggy outcrops – such as Dolwyddelan. The final wave of castle building was carried out by Edward I and was concentrated in North Wales, the idea being to create a defensive ring that would subdue the country for good.

Caernarfon Castle was meant to symbolise English dominance.

An easier way to reach the summit.

an artisan quarter and tourist cultural hotspot, together with the newly completed station for the Ffestiniog and West Highland Railway.

North of Caernarfon, at Plas Menai, lies the **National Outdoor Centre** (www.plasmenai.co.uk), which offers a host of aqua-based activities, from kayaking to windsurfing and powerboating.

Llanberis

From Caernarfon, take the A4086 east to the shores of Llyn Padarn and **Llanberis ❷**. The town's location at

Traversing the mountain on Snowdon Mountain Railway.

the foot of Snowdon and its plethora of visitor attractions ensure a brisk peak season trade, though during the winter a rather more traditional Welsh character is revealed.

Near the eastern end of Llanberis is the **Snowdon Mountain Railway** (www.snowdonrailway.co.uk; subject to weather and demand). Whether ridden in or simply watched, the little trains make a stirring sight as they leave Llanberis station and work their way up the mountain. The rack-and-pinion track was laid in an astonishing 72 days during 1895–6, using Swiss techniques, and is the only public railway of its type in the UK. Since then, increasing numbers of visitors have enjoyed the excursion – an hour each way with 30 minutes at the summit. The line runs for just over 4 miles (6km). The **Llanberis Track** up Snowdon, roughly parallel to the railway, begins from the road opposite the Royal Victoria Hotel. It is the most popular path to the summit.

Llanberis Lake Railway

The A4086 next approaches Llyn Peris and the remains of the vast hillside terraces of Dinorwig Slate

Quarries, which closed in 1969. Covering 700 acres (280 hectares) and rising some 2000ft (600m) up the flanks of Elidir Fawr, they were the largest of their kind in Britain during their heyday, employing over 3000 men. The slate was taken to Port Dinorwig (Y Felinheli) on the Menai Strait by narrow-gauge railway, now partially revived as the passenger-carrying **Llanberis Lake Railway** (www.lake-railway.co.uk). Trains leave from Gilfach Ddu station and run along the lakeside. The line is set in Padarn Country Park, an 800-acre (320-hectare) area which has numerous walking trails and boating on the lake.

The round tower of Dolbadarn castle, near Llanberis.

Beneath the slate quarries, in the original Dinorwig Quarry buildings, is the **National Slate Museum** ❸ (www.museum.wales/slate; free), where visitors can still see craftsmen cutting slate 'the old way' and are shown the gigantic waterwheel, the biggest in mainland Britain and, with a diameter of 54ft (17m), one of the biggest in the world. You can also explore former quarrymen's cottages, moved here from nearby Tanygrisiau, and see a 3D presentation on the story of slate. Near the museum is **Ropeworks Active** (www.ropeworksactive.co.uk; booking recommended), a high-level outdoor climbing centre aimed at families. The aerial challenge course has bridges, swings and a zip line.

The adjacent **Dolbadarn Castle** ❹ (www.cadw.gov.wales/visit/places-to-visit/dolbadarn-castle; free), built on a grassy knoll to guard the overland route between Caernarfon and Conwy, is today a ruin presiding over a tract of Welsh landscape ravaged and re-shaped by civilisation. The fortress, built in the thirteenth century by Llewellyn the Great, holds a grim history. Owain

Safety on Snowdon

Before setting off on any of the ascents of Snowdon, make sure you're well prepared with good walking boots, waterproofs, warm layers, map, a compass, a whistle (to attract attention in emergencies), food and water. Let someone know the route you're taking and check the weather forecast. No matter how lovely and sunny it may be at the bottom, conditions can change rapidly on the mountain.

Properly attired walkers on the summit of Snowdon.

ap Grufydd was imprisoned here for 22 years by his brother Llewellyn the Last when they were fighting for control of North Wales. Another of Llewellyn the Last's brothers, Dafydd, made Dolbadarn a base for resistance against Edward I's incursions into Wales, but the castle was seized in 1282 and Dafydd captured and executed in 1283.

Pass of Llanberis

Grey crags soar above skirts of scree and boulders close in beyond Nant Peris. With innumerable classic routes on the precipices of Glyder Fawr to the north and Snowdon to the south, the **Pass of Llanberis** ❺ has become a mecca for rock climbers. Halfway up the pass on the left soars the great prow of Dinas Cromlech. Breakthroughs in the evolution of climbing took place here with Joe Brown's ascent of Cenotaph Corner in the 1950s, Pete Livesey's Right Wall and Ron Fawcett's Fly on the Wall in the 1970s. One of the most famous routes by Joe Brown and Don Whillans was Cemetery Gates. The road (built c.1830) is narrow

and what few parking bays exist are usually occupied by climbers' vehicles. It is impossible not to be moved by the awesome scenery, even from a car, and many visitors are naturally tempted to park at **Pen-y-Pass**, 1168ft (356m). However, the car park there is notoriously over-subscribed (and expensive) so an alternative is to catch the Snowdon Sherpa bus (see page 119) up and back from Llanberis, which runs all year round. The inn at the pass, where George Mallory once stayed, is now a hotel.

Tracks to Snowdon

There are six major paths to the summit of **Snowdon** ❻ (Yr Wyddfa in Welsh). The Llanberis Path starts back in Llanberis, while starting points for the remainder will be found on this stretch of the route. Behind the car park at Pen-y-Pass begin two popular paths to Snowdon's peak 3560ft (1085m). The **Miners' Track**, the easier of the two, was constructed in 1856 to serve the Britannia Copper Mine situated high under the mountain's east face. The **Pig Track** or

The rugged Pass of Llanberis, created by two lakes cutting through the mountain pass.

Hafod Eryri, the highest building in Wales and England.

Hafod Eryri

The visitor centre on the summit of Snowdon, which officially opened in 2009, was built to replace Sir Clough Williams-Ellis' 1935 structure. Constructed in granite, in contemporary style, with expansive views from its huge glass frontage, the centre has to withstand the uncompromising weather conditions on the summit – wind speeds can reach 150mph (240kph). It offers refreshments and information on the mountain, as well as serving as the terminus for the Snowdon Mountain Railway.

'Pyg Track' (after Bwlch y Moch – Pass of the Pigs – which it crosses) is more rugged and much more challenging. Both tracks converge higher up, ascending the zig zags to join the Llanberis Path and railway for the final 300ft (90m) to the summit. The Miners' Track, as far as Llyn Llydaw, presents no difficulties and makes an enjoyable ramble. Both routes take about six hours to complete.

Cut into the steep face of Moel Berfedd and with dizzy views down Nantgwynant, the road descends to the Pen-y-Gwryd Hotel. Pen-y-Gwryd translates as 'Head of Cai's Fathomwide Pass', from Cai, one of Arthur's knights. Legend has it that Cai was large enough to block the pass with his outstretched hands. The old inn here continues to accommodate hillgoers as well as passing tourists in a style appropriate to its unique situation and history. Not only did it once host the pioneers of early British rock climbing but Everest expeditions based their training programmes here.

Turn right at the T-junction and then follow the A498 towards Beddgelert. Between Llyn Gwynant and

Llyn Dinas, a small car park at **Pont Bethania** denotes the start of Snowdon's **Watkin Path**. The path was constructed by Sir Edward Watkin, a railway engineer and early protagonist of the Channel Tunnel. Watkin Path was officially opened at a ceremony in 1892 by the great statesman, W.E. Gladstone. If you continue further up the path, there is a commemorative plaque that records: 'The Multitude sang Cymric hymns and Land of my Fathers'.

The view indicator (toposcope) on Snowdon's summit.

THE PASS OF ABERGLASLYN
By NORMAN WILKINSON P.R.I.

NORTH WALES
FOR HOLIDAYS

LONDON   MIDLAND   AND   SCOTTISH   RAILWAY

1930s poster advertising the Beddgelert area.

Beddgelert Forest Park

From Beddgelert (see page 42) continue on the A4085 Caernarfon road. Foothills to the west are clothed in the pine and larch of **Beddgelert Forest Park**. There are a number of waymarked trails for both walking and cycling. Further on lies Llyn-y-Gader, a lake mirroring the peaks along the Nantlle Ridge at its back. A little south of **Rhyd-Ddu Village** there is a car park for Snowdon's **Rhyd-Ddu Path**, one of the easier routes to the summit of Snowdon. In clear visibility almost the whole route to the peak can be seen from here.

Less than 2 miles (3km) further along the A4085 stands the Snowdon

Ranger youth hostel set above the waters of Llyn Cwellyn, home to the rare char, or red-bellied Alpine trout. It was here, on his journey through Wales in 1854, that George Borrow chatted with a local guide who offered to lead him up Snowdon and whose profession gave the **Snowdon Ranger Path**, another of the official paths to the summit, its name.

Penygroes

Instead of driving straight back to Caernarfon, you now take a less direct but more rewarding route. Turn west at Rhyd-ddu onto the B4418. Quite soon the road passes Llyn Dywarchen and squeezes through Drws-y-coed (The Wooded Pass) between the crags and scree of Craig y Bera and the menacing northern precipice of Y Garn to reach the Nantlle Valley (Dyffryn Nantlle). Passing Llyn Nantlle Uchaf, the Talysarn slate quarries and terraces of miners' cottages, you soon reach **Penygroes ❼**, with its trim chapels and memories of altogether busier times over a century ago.

Inigo Jones Slateworks

To conclude the tour, turn right along the A487, back towards Caernarfon.

Inigo Jones Slateworks.

Shop for slate

At the Inigo Jones Slateworks you can purchase all sorts of items made of fine Welsh slate, such as nameplates, plaques and even jewellery. You can pick up bags of slate chippings for the garden, and even have items made to order, such as kitchen worktops and windowsills.

Beddgelert Forest Park trail.

About a mile (1.6km) to the north, between Penygroes and Llanwnda, is the **Inigo Jones Slateworks** (www.inigojones.co.uk; charge), which dates back to 1861. Here visitors can go on self-guided tours of the workshops and browse in the showroom for a variety of slate souvenirs.

Eating Out

CAERNARFON
Black Boy Inn
Northgate St; www.black-boy-inn.com. This sixteenth-century inn is a popular place with both locals and visitors. It's a good place to visit for lunch or dinner, with a menu featuring pub favourites like honey roast ham, egg and chips, and steak and ale pie. ££

Y Gegin Fach
5–9 Pool Hill; tel: 01286 672165; closed Sun & Mon.
This cute café, with its red polka dot tablecloths, translates as the Little Kitchen and is a great place to go for a taste of Wales at very reasonable prices. Choose from full meals such as faggots or roast pork, or snacks including Welsh rarebit or spicy nachos topped with cheese. Ploughman's lunch consists of local ham and three Snowdonia cheeses. £

LLANBERIS
The Peak
86 High Street; www.thepeak restaurant.co.uk; closed Sun–Tue. This welcoming restaurant serves a varied menu featuring Eastern and Western dishes. You might find Thai fish cakes for starters, and mains like poached natural smoked haddock or Gressingham Duck breast. There are vegetarian options too. The chef, Angela Swyer, hails from London's Groucho Club fame. ££

Vaynol Arms
Nant Peris; www.robinsons brewery,com; closed Mon.
Convivial pub with lots of wood and slate that's popular with local climbers and walkers. The terrific menu sports tempting dishes like belly pork and Irish stew, perhaps with a sticky toffee pudding to rounds things off. £

WELSH LANGUAGE

Don't be surprised if you go into a shop in North Wales and find that you're unable to understand what people are saying – the ancient Celtic language of Welsh is still widely spoken here.

Beneath its veneer of tourism, Snowdonia is a stronghold of Welsh culture and tradition where one of Europe's oldest languages may be heard in everyday use. Welsh is the native tongue of a large proportion of the population, especially in the northern and western counties – and particularly around the royal town of Caernarfon; most people can speak and understand the language.

Welsh belongs to the Celtic family of languages (one of nine languages branching from what is known as Indo-European) and, as one of the Brythonic Celtic tongues, is closely related to Cornish and Breton. Its origins stem from the Celtic Iron Age people who moved into Wales from the continent between about 550 BC and AD 50. Although the language was almost certainly being spoken as early as the sixth century AD, some of the first examples of written Welsh occur in tales from the Mabinogion, a collection of mythical stories written down

A sign for Llanfair PG's full name, the longest place name in Britain.

Welsh words & phrases

Some useful phrases:

Bore da – Good morning
Nos da – Good night
Hwyl fawr – Good bye
Diolch – Thank you
Dim diolch – No thank you
Faint? – How much?
Os gwelwch chi'n dda – please
Gwely a brecwast – bed and breakfast

Some Welsh words:

Afon – river
Bara – bread
Bryn – hill
Bws – bus
Croeso – welcome
Cymraeg – Welsh
Cymru – Wales
Eglwys – church
Gwesty – hotel
Mynydd – mountain
Tafarn – pub
Ysbyty – hospital

around the thirteenth century, but of much earlier origin (see page 38).

Roman influence

During the Roman occupation, the language of the rulers had an influence on the Welsh tongue, as can be seen with words such as caws (cheese), pont (bridge) and ffenestre (window). Welsh, however, still thrived until the sixteenth-century Acts of Union ruled that English should be the only language of the courts. However, the language still survived, partly thanks to William Morgan, who translated the Bible into Welsh in 1588.

It was in the nineteenth century that the language fell into decline, due to an educational report of 1847. Written by English commissioners, it stressed the importance of the use of English, rather than Welsh, in schools. Children were forbidden to speak the language. Welsh could easily have gone the way of Cornish, and became almost a forgotten language. However, pressure groups fought to keep it alive, and, in the twenty-first century, devolution has ensured that Wales is now, officially at least, a bilingual country. Much of the country's commerce and administration is undertaken in Welsh, schools (it is a compulsory subject for pupils up to the age of 16) and road signs are bilingual and there are Welsh TV and radio channels. The National Assembly, in Cardiff, treats both English and Welsh equally.

The coast near Porthdinllaen.

TOUR 5
The Lleyn Peninsula

Running for 75 miles (121km) around the Lleyn Peninsula, this full day's tour takes you on a circuit of one of the quietest corners of North Wales; an area rich in history.

It is hard to look at a map of the Lleyn Peninsula and not be reminded of Cornwall. The western Lleyn (pronounced 'thlinn') has even been dubbed the 'Land's End of North Wales'. But over the centuries it has suffered none of Cornwall's intensive exploitation for mineral ores and china clay. Neither has it sustained so many pressures in more recent times from the holiday industry. A scattering of modest resorts the Lleyn may have, but elsewhere the landscape is hilly and agricultural. You sense, in the walled pastures and isolated farmsteads, a foreignness reminiscent of Brittany, perhaps, or southwest Ireland. It is indisputably Celtic.

The Lleyn's roads were not built for motor traffic. Narrow and twisting,

Highlights
- Criccieth
- Lloyd George Museum
- Pwllheli
- Plas Glyn-y-Weddw
- Abersoch
- Bardsey Island
- Porthdinllaen
- Llanaelhaearn
- St Beuno's Church

they meander between high banks and tall hedges with occasional sudden views of a shapely hillside or the glint of sunshine on waves. It's a great place to explore on foot or on a bicycle.

The coastline, which covers nearly 100 miles (161km) is a mostly

Criccieth's beach and thirteenth-century Criccieth Castle.

unspoilt Area of Outstanding Natural Beauty, alternating between savage cliffs and golden sands whose inaccessibility guarantees seclusion.

Criccieth

This route starts at **Criccieth ❶**, a holiday playground in Victorian times. The town's central green imparts an intimate village flavour to this essentially family resort. Almost dividing the town in half, **Criccieth** **Castle** (www.cadw.gov.wales/visit/places-to-visit/criccieth-castle; charge) perches on a grassy headland between a pebble strand backed by hotel terraces on Marine Drive and, to the east, a great arc of safe bathing beach and promenade. Visit the castle ruin if you can, both for its chequered history and for the magnificent views. Built by the Welsh in the thirteenth century, contemporary with Llewellyn the Great, it was taken by Edward I

Abersoch on the Lleyn peninsula.

who extended and refortified it, and incorporated it into his 'Iron Ring' of coastal fortifications in 1283. Owain Glyndwr's Welsh uprising besieged and sacked the castle 140 years later, leaving it much as we find it today.

Llanystumdwy

Take the A497 coast road past **Llanystumdwy** to visit its **Lloyd George Museum** ❷ (www.gwynedd. gov.uk; charge) entirely devoted to

Lloyd George Museum.

the life and times of this great Liberal politician, who was Prime Minister from 1916–22. Born in Manchester, of Welsh parents, he came to the village after his father died when he was a small child, and lived with his mother in Highgate Cottage opposite the Feathers Inn until 1880. His uncle's shoemaking workshop next door has been imaginatively re-created. Winston Churchill said of Lloyd George: 'He was the greatest Welshman which that unconquerable race has produced since the age of the Tudors'. Memorabilia on display ranges from political cartoons to the pencil with which he wrote his memoirs, and there's a film about his life. Now continue along the coast to Pwllheli.

Pwllheli

Pwllheli ❸ is the largest of the Lleyn's settlements and a market town since 1355. It was once a busy port, though it declined after the construction of Porthmadog. The marina here can berth 400 boats. Pwllheli is probably best known as the place where the Welsh National Party, Plaid Cymru, was purpose-built in the nineteenth century to house an art collection, and is today a striking art gallery with a changing collection of paintings displayed in the fine rooms. There's also a permanent collection of fine Swansea and Nantgarw porcelain and a shop where you can purchase arts and crafts.

Abersoch

Follow the coast road to **Abersoch ❺**, set in a bay called St Tudwal's Road. This and the two uninhabited offshore islands take their name from a sixth-century Brittany saint who fled from religious persecution in the Dark Ages and founded a monastic cell on St Tudwal's Island East. Ruins of an 800-year-old **chapel** there can be seen from boat trips around the islands (tel: 01758 712646; weather permitting, in season). In Abersoch itself you will find the Lleyn Peninsula's only dyed-in-the-wool holiday resort. A lively harbour, fine beach, narrow shop-lined streets, restaurants, pubs and hotels, as well as extensive complexes of caravans and chalets, all betray a wide appeal.

Llanengan to Rhiw

Head southwest on the unclassified road over to the southern end of Porth Neigwl (Hell's Mouth), above which stands the little village of

was founded in 1925. There are two beaches here: Glan y Don beach (also known as Aberech), a lovely sandy stretch to the east, and South Beach, stretching for around 3 miles (5km) to the west. They offer great bathing. Pwllheli is the northern terminus of the scenic **Cambrian Coast Railway** (www.thecambrianline.co.uk), which extends down to Aberystwyth.

Llanbedrog

Now continue following the coast, to reach **Llanbedrog**, home to **Plas Glyn-y-Weddw ❹** (www.oriel.org.uk). This Victorian Gothic mansion

Panoramas on the Lleyn

There are some wonderful viewpoints on the Lleyn. The top of Criccieth Castle is an excellent vantage point on a fine day, while Plas Glyn-y-Weddw, the Victorian mansion at Llanbedrog, offers sea views that seem to stretch forever. Then there's Plas yn Rhiw, near Abersoch, where you can look right across to Cardigan Bay.

Lleyn peninsula.

TOUR 5 — THE LLEYN PENINSULA

Beach huts at Abersoch.

Llanengan. The unrestored, twin-naved **Parish Church** dates from the fifteenth century, with roots almost a thousand years earlier. Its bells and sacred vessels were brought over from St Mary's Abbey on Bardsey Island whose pilgrims would have called at Llanengan on their journey west.

Taking the northbound by road across the Afon Soch leads to pretty Llangian hamlet. The churchyard contains a fifth- or sixth-century Roman stone bearing an inscription in Latin which declares that the

The art gallery in Plas Glyn-y-Weddw is reputedly haunted.

remains of 'Melus the Doctor, son of Martinus, lie here'. In the whole of Britain there is no other record of an early Christian burial mentioning the deceased's profession.

Bear left and left again to the northern end of Hell's Mouth, its anglicised name testimony to the threat this vast crescent bay once posed to sailing ships which risked being driven ashore in southwesterly gales. Ahead there is a steep climb to **Rhiw ⑥**, highest village on the Lleyn, where stands a delightful sixteenth-century Welsh manor house surrounded by its own grounds and ornamental garden. **Plas yn Rhiw** is owned by the National Trust (www.nationaltrust.org.uk/visit/wales/plas-yn-rhiw; charge). It was almost derelict when it was purchased in the 1930s by the Keating sisters, friends of the Welsh poet R.S. Thomas who lived in a cottage on the estate.

Aberdaron

Three miles (5km) farther west the attractive little fishing village of **Aberdaron ⑦** nestles in a fold at the back of its cliff-girt bay, sheltered from all winds but the south. In good weather there are boat trips to Bardsey Island. The final resting place for fourteenth-century pilgrims en route for Bardsey was Aberdaron's Y-Gegin-Fawr (The Big Kitchen) near the old hump-backed bridge; it is now a café. Run by the National Trust, the Porth y Swnt visitor centre (open all year) next to the bridge has information on things to see and do in the area. Recently constructed sea defences reveal Aberdaron's vulnerability to marine erosion. Note how the Norman doorway of **St Hywyn's Church** has been weathered by centuries of storms. When built some 500 years ago, it was set back at a safe distance from the shore, but now its cemetery rises incongruously from the beach and the building only survives thanks to the provision of its own sea wall.

Bardsey Island

Tentacle-like, single-track lanes reach out towards 'land's end'. For a path to the shore, go via Uwchmynydd to the end of the public road beneath the rocky fist of Mynydd Mawr. Alternatively, drive on up the concrete track to old coastguard buildings on the 524ft (160m) summit. All around the tip of the Lleyn are uninterrupted views to **Bardsey Island** (or 'Ynys Enlli', 'island of the currents' in

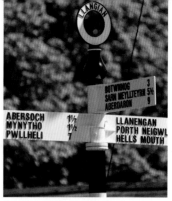

Llangian hamlet can be visited on the way from Llanengan to Rhiw.

Welsh). Founded in the sixth century, the Abbey of St Mair (St Mary) was a place of pilgrimage for hundreds of years: it was said that three pilgrimages to Bardsey were equivalent to one pilgrimage to Rome. Many holy men stayed on and were buried there, giving rise to the title 'Island of 20,000 Saints'. The abbey ruins lie beneath 548ft (167m) Mynydd Enlli, roughly in line with the lighthouse. During the early twentieth century, Bardsey was still inhabited by a fishing and farming community, but today it is largely a seabird sanctuary, visited by occasional boatloads of ornithologists bound for the observatory. Cardigan Bay down to St David's Head, the Snowdonia peaks and even, appropriately for their

Locally-caught crab for sale in Aberdaron.

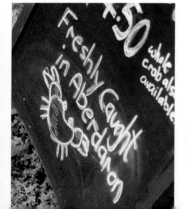

Boat trips to Bardsey

Various operators offer boat trips to Bardsey Island. You can take a trip on Highlander II with Enlli Charter (www.enllicharter.co.uk), who operate from Pwllheli and incorporate dolphin, porpoise, whale and bird watching. Bardsey Boat Trips run half-hour trips from Aberdaron (www.bardseyboattrips.com), landing on the island for four hours to appreciate its wildlife and serenity.

Morfa Nefyn.

shared Celtic heritage, the Wicklow Mountains of Ireland, can be seen from high ground.

Porthdinllaen

Return to Aberdaron and follow the B4413 northeast to Pen-y-groeslon. Here turn left on the B4417 to Tudweiliog. Continue along the B4417 to **Morfa Nefyn**, where there's a National Trust car park. It's best to park here and walk the mile (1.6km) or so of track to the hamlet of **Porthdinllaen ❽**, acquired by the National Trust in 1994. The

Nant Gwrtheryn.

picturesque sandy cove backed by neat cottages and a waterfront pub had once been earmarked as the packet port for Ireland. In 1806 William Madocks, Member of Parliament for Boston, Lincolnshire, formed a company to build a harbour at Porthdinllaen, but two years later when the necessary Parliamentary Bill was introduced it failed to gain support and Holyhead was selected instead. Madocks' ambition resurfaced in 1844 when Porthdinllaen established its own railway company. However, the Chester and Holyhead line, already built, proved the decisive factor in the final abandonment of Madocks' scheme and Porthdinllaen sank into quiet obscurity. Only Madocks' straight road to Pwllheli, designed for speeding transit of the Irish mail, and his development of Porthmadog and Tremadog as staging posts on the route to London (see page 44) remain.

Nant Gwrtheryn

Continue on the B4417 through Nefyn to Llithfaen. A mile (1.6km) to the north at **Nant Gwrtheryn** is the **Welsh Language Centre** (www.nantgwrtheryn.org), housed in a once-derelict quarry village, even today a wild and remote spot. There are fabulous views and an excellent café. **Llanaelhaearn** ❾ is a small village at the foot of Lleyn's three most distinctive peaks known as *Yr Eifl* (The Forks), or by their English name The Rivals. The highest, central top reaches 1850ft (564m), the lowest, to seaward, 1457ft (444m). But it is the eastern peak that holds the greatest interest, for its summit is crowned by the remains of Tre'r Ceiri (Town of the Giants). This ancient, fortified settlement, probably of Bronze Age origin and containing well-preserved hut circles, can be reached by a footpath off the B4417 less than a mile (1.6km) southwest of Llanaelhaearn.

St Beuno's Church

Bear north along the coast on the A499, to reach **Clynnog-fawr** to visit the surprisingly large fifteenth-century church of **St Beuno** ❿, which stands on the site of a seventh-century monastery. Inside is a medieval wooden chest, a reminder that the church was once an important stopping point on the pilgrim route to Bardsey Island.

Now turn south on the A499, follow it for a while then turn left onto the B4354 through Chwilog, to visit **Penarth Fawr** (www.cadw.gov/wales; free) a fifteenth-century hall house that belonged to a wealthy family. It's noted for its fine timber roof. Afterwards, you can now return to Criccieth.

Eating Out

CRICCIETH
Cadwaladers
Castle Street; www.cadwaladers.co.uk. The flagship of the renowned ice-cream makers, this bright and breezy café is also open for brunch, coffee, light lunches and more; terrific sea views from the raised balcony. £

PWLLHELI
Y Bryncynan
Morfa Nefyn, nr Pwllheli; www.ybryncynan.pub.
A family and dog-friendly inn with an extensive menu ranging from steaks to burgers. There are pub favourites like cottage pie and steak and ale pie, as well as ploughmans' and sandwiches. ££

Whitehall
Stryd Moch, www.whitehall.cymru. This picturesque gastropub is set in a Grade II-listed whitewashed cottage dating back to 1818, but with modern renovations. The food is well-presented and ranges from the likes of creamy fish pie on the lunch menu

and a ballotine of chicken wrapped in bacon on the dinner menu. £££

LLANBEDROG
Poachers Restaurant
66–68 High Street; www.poachersrestaurant.uk; closed Sun–Tues.
This contemporary restaurant serves dishes such as Hungarian-style pork goulash and cod fillets with tiger prawns. For dessert try their baked lemon cheesecake. The menu changes with the seasons and there are vegetarian choices available. ££

Tremfan Hall
Tremfan Hall; www.tremfanhall.co.uk. Lovely country house overlooking Tremadog Bay, offering a varied menu of modern British dishes. Choices might include starters of Menai oysters or langoustine bisque, followed by slow braised Welsh beef shoulder steak or sweet potato & vegetables in coconut curry sauce. For dessert you might find *crème brûlée* or pecan pie. £££

Portmeirion.

TOUR 6

Tremadog Bay to the Mawddach Estuary

This 53-mile (85km) one-day circuit takes you to the fantasy village of Portmeirion and picturesque Harlech Castle, along the coast to Barmouth and then inland.

On this route you reach the southern parts of Snowdonia National Park. Ardudwy, the high and ancient upland region between the Vale of Ffestiniog and the Mawddach estuary, guards its secrets well. Many of the Mabinogion's heroic sagas are based here. Ireland, just across the sea, seems to have a presence, visible in the primeval stones named *cyttiau wyddelod* – Irishman's huts. Modern roads only tickle the foothills and it is rough country to walk in. In his book *On Foot in North Wales*, published in 1933, Patrick Monkhouse writes about an ascent of Rhinog Fawr: 'it exacts more perspiration to the yard than any other mile in Wales…'. This is where experienced local walkers come

Highlights

- Portmeirion
- Harlech Castle
- Morfa Harlech Nature Reserve
- Llandanwg Church
- Barmouth
- Mawddach Estuary
- Cymer Abbey

when they want to escape the crowds. Fortunately, the coastline is a softer place with dunes and sandy beaches extending all the way to Barmouth, a classic holiday resort. Watching over the seas is Harlech Castle, which juts defiantly skyward.

Portmeirion

Your route starts in Porthmadog, terminus for the vintage Ffestiniog Railway (see page 45). Shortly after crossing The Cob, take the driveway on the right to **Portmeirion** ❶ (www.portmeirion.wales; charge), a folly par excellence which draws in visitors from across the globe. Following a tour of Italy when he became captivated by the fishing village of Portofino, the architect Clough Williams-Ellis searched for a suitable site on which to create an Italianate fantasy of his own. In 1925, quite by chance, he was offered the present land, then derelict, beside the Dwyryd Estuary not far from his ancestral home. Work began in 1926, with the village developing around an Italian-style piazza, and dotted with arches, statues and fountains. His declared mission was to 'show that one could develop even a very beautiful place without defiling it and, given sufficient care, you could even enhance what was given as a backdrop'. Williams-Ellis always intended Portmeirion to awaken visitors' interest in architecture, decor and landscaping. In amongst the extravaganza of small-scale, pastel-coloured Mediterranean buildings, including shops and cafés, appear architectural oddments from all over Britain, some rescued from demolition sites by Williams-Ellis himself.

The nineteenth-century house standing on the original site became the Portmeirion Hotel which hosted many celebrities during the 1930s. Bernard Shaw and John Steinbeck stayed there, as did the playwright Noël Coward, who wrote *Blithe Spirit* here. Castell Deudraeth, a Victorian mansion on the estate, was built for a local MP. Williams-Ellis purchased it and used it as a hotel for a while in the 1930s; it now once again functions as a high-end hotel

Views around Italianate village of Portmeirion.

Portmeirion was the main location for cult 1960s TV series, *The Prisoner*, and still attracts many fans, culminating in the annual Prisoner convention. There are walks above the sandy shoreline backed by 70 acres (28 hectares) of subtropical gardens as well as through woodland to little bays on the peninsula's south side (strong tidal currents make bathing dangerous). On a fine day it would be easy to spend a whole day here.

Llandecwyn Church

Return to the A487 and fork right opposite Penrhyndeudraeth's church to pass the railway station on the scenic Cambrian Coast Line between Pwllheli and Aberystwyth (see page 65). In fact, the road curves across the Afon Dwyryd beside the railway line on the Pont Briwet to Llandecwyn station before heading for the lake-dotted foothills north of the main Rhinog range, encountered more closely later. Rather than following

Llandecwyn Church.

the A496 south, stay on this byroad via Bryn Bwbach. Up to the left, halfway between the two Tecwyn lakes, stands the isolated little **Llandecwyn Church**, which has medieval origins and is also a magnificent viewpoint. Resuming your southerly progress, fork right after a couple of miles at Eisingrug, to reach the B4573.

Alternatively, for superb panoramas over Tremadog Bay, stay on the narrow mountain road climbing the shoulder of Moel Goedog, 1211ft (369m), an area rich in prehistoric remains. Either way, the next port of call will be Harlech.

Harlech

At one time **Harlech ❷** was a fashionable coastal resort, attracting famous people such as the composer Gustav Holst, the poet Robert Graves, Sir Henry Wood (of the Proms) and George Bernard Shaw. It's even said that nude bathing began here in the 1930s. The town is small, so easy to explore, and very attractive with winding streets. It makes a good base for walks and drives in this part of Snowdonia – and golfers will love its 18-hole, par 69, internationally renowned links golf course, Royal St David's.

Harlech Castle (www.cadw.gov. wales; charge) entirely dominates the little hillside town. Designated a UNESCO World Heritage Site, its square-cut profile atop a 200ft (60m) -high crag is visible from many miles distant.

Work on the castle began in 1283, after Edward I's conquest of Wales.

Darwin's inspiration

As a child, Charles Darwin spent many family holidays in North Wales, and became a keen collector of the shells, fossils and insects that he found there. It sparked a lifelong interest in natural history. While a student at Cambridge, he travelled to North Wales and visited Barmouth, collecting beetles and studying its geology. The skills and knowledge he acquired were to serve him well when he took up his place on the voyage of the *Beagle*.

Darwin studied the geology of Capel Curig and Caernarfon.

It was part of his iron ring of castles that was built to subdue and defend the area: each castle was within a day's march of another. Around 950 men carried out the work and the castle was completed in 1283. In 1290, as a reward for his work building this and other fortifications, James of St George, Edward I's Master of Works, became Constable of Harlech in 1290. Under his direction, Harlech Castle was given four massive towers,

anchoring the great curtain walls. A huge gatehouse, rather than the more usual central keep, formed the building's strongest section. The Castle's position directly above a tidal creek (the sea has since receded about half a mile/800m) permitted victualling from the sea, and supplies from Ireland were carried up the west-side steps which still exist today.

Harlech Castle.

Imposing entrance to Harlech Castle.

Despite its apparent impregnability, the castle fell to Owain Glyndwr in 1404, who held a parliament here in 1405. It was recaptured by the English within five years, but then played a starring role in the Wars of the Roses when it was held by the Lancastrians. The castle was besieged by Yorkist troops (the numbers estimated at between 7000 and 10,000 men) and subsequently surrendered; the siege is thought to have inspired the now famous marching song *Men of Harlech*. The castle's battlements offer superb views across the sea and over to Snowdon.

Morfa Harlech

Harlech overlooks 5 miles (8km) of dune-backed sandy beach and an expanse of reclaimed land – **Morfa Harlech** – part of which is a nature reserve. It is home to rare plants and insects that live on such soft dunes, including the Welsh mudwort, lizards and the rare mining bee. Birds such as redshank and wigeon may be spotted, while otters and water voles use nearby estuarine waterways. The reserve is west of Harlech on the A496. There's a car park, and a footpath leads to the sands.

The Rhinogs

In complete contrast, a narrow mountain road to the east snakes uphill into Cwm Bychan where, from the road-end car park, an ascent may be made to the so-called Roman Steps (research suggests the paved way is more likely to have been a medieval packhorse route). **Rhinog** terrain – rocks and boulders concealed beneath deep heather – is notoriously rugged. Any attempt to scale Rhinog Fawr, 2362ft (720m), should only be made by experienced and well-equipped hillwalkers. These are, however, splendidly wild hills, a landscape of boggy hollows, bare cliffs, knobbly ridge crests and high, lonely lakes. There are only two ways cross the range: Bwlch Tyddiad with its Roman steps and Bwlch Drws Ardudwy to the south, and neither path is open to vehicular traffic – in poor weather it can be an intimidating place.

Llandanwg Church

South of Harlech, a right turn off the A496 at Llanfair leads to the fourth-century **Llandanwg Church** ❸. Dedicated to St Tanwg, this extraordinary church is one of the very earliest places of worship in Wales. The present building is early medieval and was used until the mid-nineteenth century. Abandoned, it was invaded by drifting dunes, and it was not until the 1980s that it was restored. The nearby **Llanfair Slate Caverns** (www.llanfairslatecaverns. co.uk; charge) offer an interesting diversion and there is a Farm Park (May–Sept) that will be of interest to children. Further south on the A496 is **Llanbedr** ❹ where a tidal causeway

Wales currently has a record 45
beaches with Blue Flag status.

Blue Flag bathing

Many of the beaches in North Wales
have been awarded Blue Flag
status, a scheme which judges them
annually for criteria such as water
quality and litter management. It
means that children can be assured
of safe, clean bathing. Amongst those
beaches with Blue Flag status are
beaches at Llandudno, Abersoch,
Criccieth, Barmouth, Prestatyn,
Pwllheli and Church Bay on Anglesey.

leads out to **Shell Island**, or Mochras,
an exposed, low-lying peninsula with
a campsite, marina and over 200
varieties of shell deposited by unusual
offshore currents. Inland, again,
another narrow mountain road with
picnic spots approaches the Rhinogs
via Cwm Nantcol.

Never far from the railway line, the
A496 proceeds south past Dyffryn
Ardudwy and Tal-y-bont, nudged ever
nearer the sandy shore by high ground
until from Llanaber everything crowds
cheek-by-jowl into the only usable

corridor of land. Follow the road to
reach **Barmouth** ❺.

Barmouth

Barmouth's Welsh name, Abermaw,
a contraction of Aber-mawddach
(Estuary of the Mawddach), dates back
to its humble origins as a fishing port
and boatyard. When the railway came
in the mid-nineteenth century, the
village's extensive sandy beach and its
incomparable views over the estuary
to Cadair Idris quickly earned it a
reputation as a holiday resort.

Morfa Harlech.

View of Cadair Idris from Barmouth.

Four and a half acres (1.8 hectares) of cliffland above the town – **Dinas Oleu** (Fortress of Light) – represents the National Trust's very first acquisition; it was presented by Mrs F. Talbot in 1895, the year of the Trust's foundation, and a further 12 acres (4.8 hectares) were added to it in 1980. It is well signposted, and a little further east will be found the waymarked Panorama Walk providing views not only of Cadair Idris and the coast but inland over the estuary's head to the distant Aran mountains.

It is also possible to cross the railway line's timber viaduct spanning the Mawddach (always a vulnerable section of the Cambrian Coast Line and expensive to maintain) using the pedestrian walkway. Additionally a seasonal ferry runs across to the narrow-gauge Fairbourne Steam Railway on the far shore (see page 103). Walkers and cyclists can join the **Mawddach Trail** (www.mawddach trail.co.uk) in Barmouth. This crosses over the estuary, then runs for 9.5 miles (15km) along a disused railway line to Dolgellau.

In this region of mid-Wales the happy juxtaposition of railway stations and superb walking country opens up numerous possibilities for returning to the start of rambles by train.

Ty Crwn and Ty Gwyn

Just in from Barmouth Harbour stands **Ty Crwn**, a circular 'lock-up' built in the early nineteenth century to accommodate, among other offenders, drunken goldminers from the Bontddu area just upstream. There are reminders of Barmouth's maritime heritage at **Ty Gwyn**, a medieval tower house, where finds from local shipwrecks are displayed. The building is said to have been where Jaspar Tudor, Earl of Pembroke, plotted against Richard III. It was a campaign which resulted in Richard's defeat at the battle of Bosworth at the hands of Jaspar's nephew, Henry Tudor, who took the Crown and became Henry VII in 1485, starting the Tudor dynasty.

In June of each year Barmouth sees the start of the **Three Peaks International Yacht Race** (www.three peaksyachtrace.co.uk) during which

Royalty has been wearing Welsh
gold since the early 1920s.

competitors sail to Fort William,
climbing en route to the summits
of Snowdon, Scafell Pike and Ben
Nevis. And if the resort's present-day
ambience is of 'sandcastles, donkey
rides and candy floss', at least there is
ample car parking and plenty of space
for everyone.

Mawddach Estuary

Your route now goes inland, as the
A496 bears east and traces the tree-clad
northern shore of the Afon Mawddach
and into former gold territory. The
Welsh Gold Rush began around 1850
with the discovery of the precious
yellow metal at Clogau on the western
edge of the so-called Dolgellau Gold

Belt which stretched in a wide arc from
Bala in the east to **Bontddu** ❻ on the
Mawddach estuary. After a highly
profitable period between 1904 and
1906, production steadily declined and
Clogau closed in 1911. The fenced-off
entrance to the Clogau St David's gold
mine can still be seen today, to the west
of a lane running up from Bontddu
beside the Hirgwm stream. The
wedding rings of the Queen Mother
(1923), the Queen (1947), Princess
Margaret (1960), Princess Anne (1973)
and Diana, Princess of Wales (1981)
were all crafted from the same nugget
of Welsh gold found there. Continuing

Boats on Mawddach estuary.

The ruins of Cymer Abbey.

with tradition the Duchess of Cornwall (2005) and the Duchess of Cambridge (2011) also chose wedding rings made of Welsh gold.

Cymer Abbey

Near Llanelltyd further east along the estuary, the New Precipice Walk skirts the slopes of Foel Ispri 1000ft (321m) above the Afon Mawddach. The better-known Precipice Walk begins further east from car parking near Llyn Cynwch (see page 97). See also the modest but evocative remains nearby of **Cymer Abbey** ❼ (daily), founded in 1198 and one of the major Cistercian foundations supported by the Princes of Gwynedd. The ruins are mainly those of the uncompleted thirteenth-century abbey church.

Trawsfynydd and Tomen-y-mur

Across the river to the right stands Dolgellau, but you follow the A470 as it forks left at Llanelltyd and climbs back to the north, towards the starting point of the route through the Coed-

y-Brenin forest. More details on this magnificent forest are given in Tour 8, but even if you're only passing it's still worth calling in at the Coed-y-Brenin Visitor Centre to the right of the main road. You can pick up details of walks and forest bicycle trails there, and there's a handy café too.

The road strikes due north to by-pass **Trawsfynydd** ❽ village, with the Rhinog mountains – the heights of Ardudwy – ranged along the

Afon Mawddach from the Precipice Walk.

western skyline. From Trawsfynydd, it is possible to do a circular walk of around 3 hours to visit **Tomen-y-mur**, the site of a Roman fort built around AD 78 and occupied until AD 140. There are the remains of a bathhouse and possibly an amphitheatre. After the Romans left, it was later built on by the Normans. Details of the circular walk route are on the Snowdonia National Park website (www.snowdonia.gov.wales). Bwlch Drws Ardudwy forms a conspicuous notch, while the highest top, Y Llethr (1875ft/756m), lies at the southern end of the massif. The waters of Llyn Trawsfynydd were once warmed by the reactors of the nuclear power station, which closed in 1991 and is still being decommissioned.

Ignore the A470's right turn to Llan Ffestiniog and branch left at Gellilydan on a by-road over to Maentwrog in the beautiful Vale of Ffestiniog (see page 47). Parallel to the Ffestiniog Railway which threads unseen but often heard through the forest above, the A487 heads towards Porthmadog via Penrhyndeudraeth, headquarters of the Snowdonia National Park.

Eating Out

HARLECH
Castle Cottage Inn
Y Llech; www.castlecottageinn harlech.com; Fri & Sat evening only; booking essential.
This Michelin-recommended restaurant with rooms is in the centre of Harlech. The menu changes with the seasons, and features lots of local fish (perhaps there'll be a Barmouth lobster bisque for a starter), Welsh beef, lamb and Carmarthen ham. Desserts might include an imaginative banana and rum strudel. £££

BARMOUTH
Bistro Bermo
Church Street; www.thebistro bermo.com; closed Sun–Tues.
Welsh produce is used at this intimate bistro, sometimes with a Spanish twist. Starters might include smoked salmon or king prawns, while typical main courses include succulent steaks or vegetarian Wellington. The monkfish with lightly curried mussels is a triumph. ££

Foxglove
Staffordshire House, www.foxglove barmouth.co.uk; closed Mon–Wed.
Exceptional vegan restaurant offering a five-course set menu of organically and locally-sourced products and foraged food. – and you certainly don't need to be vegan to appreciate the quality of the cuisine here. ££

Ty'r Graig Castle
Llanaber Road; www.tyrgraig-castle.co.uk.
Perched high above Barmouth, with great views over Cardigan Bay, is this striking Victorian building. Originally a family home, it is now an hotel with grand Victorian interiors. The restaurant serves a range of dishes such as sautéed king prawns, poached cod steak, Welsh beef, and also some vegetarian choices. They also serve afternoon tea. ££

Wilderness café
Castle Square; www.facebook.com/ ygwyllt.harlech.
Dog-friendly café in the heart of Harlech with indoor and outdoor seating.
Even those without a sweet tooth will struggle to resist their decadent cakes and sweet treats. Serving hot drinks, soups, sandwiches and pizza with vegan options available. This cosy, quirky café also boasts an on-site gift shop selling soaps, trinkets and more. ££

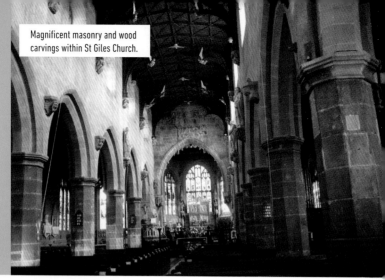

Magnificent masonry and wood carvings within St Giles Church.

TOUR 7

Wrexham to Bala – and Back

This full day's tour of 116 miles (186km) starts in Wrexham, close to the border with England, then heads to Llangollen and on to the countryside around Bala Lake.

Wrexham became prosperous in the eighteenth century when minerals were discovered in the surrounding countryside. It is not on the main tourist trail, but it does boast a fine church, while Llangollen, in contrast, attracts many visitors who come to enjoy the annual International Musical Eisteddfod. This corner of North Wales offers some unexpected scenic beauties, like the gloriously pastoral Ceiriog Valley. Further on, there is an unexpected wildness reminiscent of the northern Pennines of England. Villages and farmsteads cling to the edges of this 'empty quarter'. Mist often clings to its high ground, adding moisture to an already wet landscape of bog and lakes, of tumbling streams and waterfalls. Exploration on foot is not easy, but a

few mountain roads do transect the area, providing an opportunity to experience the roof of Snowdonia from the security of a vehicle.

Highlights

- St Giles Church, Wrexham
- Erddig Hall
- Plas Newydd
- Valle Crucis Abbey
- Bala Lake
- Llyn Celyn
- The Migneint

Wrexham

The tour begins in **Wrexham ❶** at the town's most famous landmark, the 136ft (41m) Gothic tower of

Wrexham's markets

Every Monday in Wrexham there's a large outdoor market in Queen's Square, with stalls selling everything from fruit and vegetables to clothes and carpets. Wrexham Country Markets, with its origins in the Women's Institute, hold a market every Friday (9.30am–2pm) in Wingetts Sale Room, Holt Street, selling home-made cakes, preserves, crafts and plants.

Wrexham is home to North Wales' largest market.

St Giles Church (Castle Street; www.st gilesparishchurchwrexham.org.uk), which is considered one of the 'Seven Wonders of Wales'. The interior of the fifteenth-century church contains fine stained glass, including a window attributed to Burne-Jones, and traces of a fifteenth-century wall painting of the Last Judgement. The town also has a **museum** (www.wrexhamheritage.wales; charge), which is soon to be joined by a Football Museum for Wales. The Clywedog Trail, a 9-mile (14km) waymarked walking trail gives an insight into Wrexham's industrial past.

Erddig Hall

Leave Wrexham in a southerly direction on the A483, exit at junction 3, then follow signposts on minor roads to reach **Erddig Hall** ❷ (www.nationaltrust.org.uk/visit/wales/erddig; charge). This eighteenth-century mansion, set in extensive grounds, offers a fascinating glimpse of the 'upstairs-downstairs' aspects of country-house life. In the family's grand rooms, visitors can see fine furniture, paintings and textiles, which contrast with the servants' quarters and kitchens 'below stairs'.

Erddig Hall.

Chirk and the Ceiriog Valley

Rejoin the A483 and continue heading south. After 7 miles (11km), at a roundabout, join the A5 towards Llangollen, then in a short distance join the B5070 to **Chirk**. Two miles (3km) west of Chirk, just beyond Chirk Station, is **Chirk Castle ❸** (www.nationaltrust.org.uk/visit/wales/chirk-castle; charge). It looks like a grand stately home, but was built around 1295, during the reign of Edward I and with his royal approval. Work finished around 1310. The castle changed hands several times until, in 1595, it was purchased by Sir Thomas Myddelton, a London merchant who made it into a comfortable family home. The state rooms boast the fine furniture and paintings you'd expect from a grand house, while the extensive parkland is well worth exploring.

From Chirk, you can opt to make a wonderfully scenic drive along the B4500, which winds through the pastoral countryside of the **Ceiriog Valley** (Glyn Ceiriog). You can follow the road all the way to Llanarmon

Enthusiasts preserved and reopened the railway after its closure.

Dyffryn Ceiriog (bearing left on an unclassified road at The Hand public house, which includes an attractive inn). It's about 11 miles (18km) from Chirk. Return the same route to Chirk to rejoin the main drive and go west on the A5 to reach Llangollen.

Llangollen

Llangollen ❹ is a lively market town on the River Dee, surrounded

Llangollen Canal.

by picturesque scenery. It's a popular centre for people on narrow-boat holidays, as the **Llangollen Canal** runs through town, part of Thomas Telford's Pontcysyllte Aqueduct. Railway fans will want to take a journey on the **Llangollen Railway** (www.llangollen-railway.co.uk; charge) a steam railway which runs for 10 miles (16km) from Llangollen station to Corwen, alongside the river.

Plas Newydd

Llangollen's most famous sight is **Plas Newydd** (Hill Street; www.denbighshire.gov.uk; charge), the former home of Sarah Ponsonby and Lady Eleanor Charlotte Butler, an eighteenth-century lesbian couple who eloped together, set up home and became known as the Ladies of Llangollen. They lived together for 50 years and became quite a tourist attraction in their lifetime, receiving distinguished visitors ranging from the Duke of Wellington and Sir Walter Scott to Josiah Wedgwood and William Wordsworth. Their house, a fairly simple cottage when they bought it, was transformed over the years into an overpowering Gothic creation. Inside is an exhibition on their lives, while their bedchamber has been furnished to look much as it did at the end of their lives.

Valle Crucis Abbey

Around 1.5 miles (2.5km) outside Llangollen, on the A542, are the romantic ruins of **Valle Crucis Abbey** (www.cadw.gov.wales/visit/places-to-visit/valle-crucis-abbey; charge with free entry for disabled persons and companions), a Cistercian house

Ruins of Valle Crucis Abbey.

founded in 1201. At that time this would have been an extremely isolated spot, ideal for contemplation. You can still feel the grandeur of the building, which was deserted after the Dissolution in the sixteenth century – and can even see the monks' fishpond.

Bala

Take the A5 from Llangollen, driving through Corwen, shortly after which you turn left to join the A494 to reach **Bala ⑤**, in Snowdonia National Park. Bala was a prosperous centre of the woollen industry prior to the Industrial Revolution. Thomas Pennant wrote of women and children 'in full employ, knitting along the roads'. But, the town's reputation as a religious centre proved more enduring. There is a statue to Thomas Charles, pioneer of Welsh Calvinistic Methodism and a leader of the Sunday School movement.

Bala Lake

Bala Lake (Llyn Tegid) constitutes the largest natural area of water in Wales, being about 4 miles (6.4km) long by 0.75 mile (1.2km) wide and with

a maximum depth of around 136ft (48m). Because of its situation in the great rift valley extending southwest to Tal-y-lyn and the sea at Tywyn – a natural through-route from the Vale of Chester – many travellers have written of the lake, its prodigious fish population (including the unique alpine gwyniad) and the fine sailing to be had upon its waters.

Hauled by narrow-gauge steam and diesel engines, the **Bala Lake Railway** (www.bala-lake-railway.co.uk; check timetable) carries visitors for 9 miles (14km) along the scenic eastern shore of the lake between Bala and the village of Llanuwchllyn – the birthplace of Michael Jones, a prominent Welsh Nationalist who initiated Welsh settlement in Patagonia.

To the southeast of Llanuwchllyn, an impressive mountain road climbing to Bwlch y Groes is well worth the detour. This is Wales's highest road pass at 1790ft (546m), giving access to the mighty Aran Mountains before dropping to Dinas Mawddwy (see page 96). A similarly high-level road heads west from Llanuwchllyn. At

From Wales to Patagonia

In the mid-nineteenth century, as the pressure to speak English increased, moves were made to protect the language by moving overseas. A Welsh nationalist non-conformist, Michael D. Jones, who lived near Bala, put forward the idea of establishing a community in Patagonia. He finally got together around 150 Welsh speakers, who left from Liverpool in 1865. The community still exists today.

The Eisteddfod in Patagonia celebrates Welsh culture.

Pen-y-bont, 300yds/m after joining the northbound A494, turn left beside the Afon Lliw. In about 1.5 miles (2.5km) the road crosses the river at Dolhendre and begins a long ascent into wild open country before recrossing the Afon Lliw to reach its highest point at 1742ft (531m) above sea level. Travellers should note, however, that while spectacular, the route does involve the opening and closing of numerous gates. Passing through forestry and accompanying the Afon Gain for a mile (1.6km) or so lower down, the route swings northwest to meet the A470 near Trawsfynydd (see page 78).

National White Water Centre

A much easier road to the west, also joining the A470 near Trawsfynydd, is the A4212 from Bala, via Llyn Celyn, a large reservoir. Just beyond the junction with the B4501 at Frongoch, to the left of the main road, is the **National White Water Centre** (www.national whitewatercentre.co.uk). Although whitewater rafting is the main course of action here, if you don't want to then you can enjoy their woodland walking trail, picnic spots or café beside the Afon Tryweryn. The centre also offers canyoning and canoeing.

Bala Lake.

Rhaeadr y Cwm, Rhaeadr Cynfal.

A drowned village

Not so many years ago **Llyn Celyn** ❻ itself was just a marshy valley containing the long-established community of Capel Celyn and the old railway line from Blaenau Ffestiniog to Bala. During the 1960s – a time of momentous environmental decisions, not least the building of Trawsfynydd nuclear power station – the Afon Tryweryn was dammed to form Llyn Celyn as a holding reservoir for Liverpool Corporation. Despite much public opposition, the village of Capel Celyn, with its school, post office, chapel and farms, was drowned. Many of the community subsequently emigrated to Pennsylvania, and they and the village are remembered by a bronze plaque set on a boulder just beyond the grass-covered dam, and in a restored chapel at the lake's northwestern end. Continue on the A4212 road to Llyn Trawsfynydd.

Rhaeadr Cynfal

A mile (1.6km) beyond the decommissioned nuclear power station on the shore of Llyn Trawsfynydd, turn right with the A470 towards **Llan Ffestiniog** ❼, a large village of terraced stone houses situated some way south of the main slate quarries which take its name. Blaenau Ffestiniog lies 3 miles (5km) to the north (see page 47). Near the old railway station a footpath that leads to **Rhaeadr Cynfal**, (Cynfal Falls). Another fine waterfall on the Afon Cynfal – Rhaeadr y Cwm – can be reached on foot 1.5 miles (2.5km) upstream from Bont Newydd.

The Migneint

At Llan Ffestiniog turn right onto the B4391, the old, pre-power station road from Porthmadog to Bala. Soon after passing a superb viewpoint into the Cynfal ravine, take a left turn onto the B4407. In every direction the land rolls out into bog and heather moorland. This is the **Migneint** ❽ (Swampy Place). The often-saturated hillsides of reeds and peat hags, where acid ground has encouraged the growth of mat-grass, cotton-grass and deer's hair-sedge, represent the most significant area of such terrain in Wales. Walkers venturing forth have to contend with pools of black water, very soggy going and in all likelihood the need to navigate by compass in the frequent mists. Little wonder it is so little visited. Nevertheless, the Migneint is extremely important ecologically. Large tracts have been acquired by the

National Trust and designated a Site of Special Scientific Interest.

The ribbon of tarmac winds over this desolate, lake-dotted wilderness, home to birds like golden plovers, snipe, grouse and curlew, and in about 3 miles (5km), at Pont ar Conwy, crosses the infant River Conwy not far from its source in Llyn Conwy. To the southeast rises the peak of Arenig Fach (2261ft/689m), while downstream is the sleepy village of Ysbyty Ifan, centre of the National Trust's large Penrhyn Estate.

Fork right on an unclassified road over the River Conwy, continuing to **Pentrefoelas** ❾ on the A5. After the village of Nebo, the B5421 branches off to Llanrwst (see page 22), but just beyond this fork in the road is a lay-by offering stunning views down into the Conwy Valley and up to the distant summits of Snowdonia.

Back on the A5, bypass Rhydlydan and continue to Cerrigydrudion. You may wish to extend this tour by turning right onto the B4501 Bala Road 1 mile (1.6km) south of the village. Once across the Afon Ceirw, this climbs over to the Afon Medrad valley before swinging west and south to Frongoch and back to Bala. Otherwise continue on the A5 to return to Llangollen, after which you bear north on the A483 to reach Wrexham again.

Eating Out

NR WREXHAM
Pant-yr-Ochain
Old Wrexham Road, Gresford; www.brunningandprice.co.uk/pantyrochain
A lovely sixteenth-century manor house, set in pretty gardens, that is now an inn. The menu features mouthwatering dishes such as hoi sin oyster mushroom bao bun and slow braised lamb ragout, while desserts might include glazed lemon tart or triple chocolate brownie. ££

NR CHIRK
The West Arms Hotel
Llanarmon Dyffyn-Ceiriog; www.thewestarms.com.
Sitting at the heart of the scenic Ceiriog Valley, this inn boasts plenty of atmosphere with log fires, low ceilings and a cosy bar. The lunch menu includes sandwiches and small plates, while evening dishes might include classic comforts like vegan burgers and chef's pie of the day. They also serve Sunday lunch (noon–2.30pm). Afterwards, wind down at the bar by the crackling fireplace. ££

LLANGOLLEN
The Corn Mill
Dee Lane; www.brunningand price.co.uk/cornmill.
On fine days you can sit outside on the decked area beside the river at this lovely, converted corn mill in Llangollen. The corn mill dates back to the thirteenth century, so it's a historic site too. As well as a good selection of light meals, you can enjoy mains such as chicken, ham and leek pie, or steak burger, and maybe lemon cheesecake and profiteroles for dessert. ££

NR CORWEN
Tyddan Llan
Llandrillo; www.tyddynllan.co.uk, booking essential.
The menu at this first-rate restaurant, set in the countryside near Corwen, reflects the best of Welsh produce, and changes frequently. There are two- and three-course set menus and an eight-course tasting menu serving delights like griddled scallops with cauliflower purée, and spiced lamb with aubergine and kofta; vegetarians can be catered for with notice. £££

SNOWDONIA NATIONAL PARK

Designated in 1951, the Snowdonia National Park sits in the ancient Welsh region of Gwynedd covering 823 sq miles (2132 sq km). It is home to the famous mountain, Snowdon.

The National Park encompasses nine mountain ranges, with 90 peaks over 2000ft (609m), and 15 over 3000ft (914m). Add to these the many lakes, waterfalls, forests and soft green valleys – plus an extensive coastline etched with beaches of the softest sand – and you have a landscape of extraordinary variety. Snowdonia also has a complex geology, and fossil shell fragments

found on the summit of Snowdon are a reminder that 500 million years ago the top of this mountain was part of the sea bed.

Snowdonia's wildlife is wonderfully rich, and some species are unique to the area – notably arctic alpine plants like the Snowdon lily, and the brightly coloured Snowdon beetle. In Llyn Tegid (Bala Lake), the largest natural

Majestic Snowdon.

lake in the National Park, there's even a type of fish known as the gwyniad, which was trapped in the deep waters at the end of the last Ice Age and has evolved into a distinct subspecies.

Rare wildlife

The lake is also home to the marvellously named glutinous snail, a freshwater snail that requires pollution-free water that is rich in calcium to thrive, a habitat that is no longer easy to find, making the snail one of the rarest in Europe. Other invertebrates to be found in Snowdonia include several butterflies: the small silver-studded blue, the endangered glorious gold and orange-hued marsh fritillary, and the large heath butterfly.

There is a fragile population of freshwater pearl mussels as well. These little mussels, which like to live in fast-running cool water, can live for up to 100 years and are noted for producing dark coloured pearls. Birdwatchers have the chance of spotting black grouse, golden plovers, nightjars and skylarks. It is the range of habitats that is so important, and Snowdonia has precious woodlands and wetlands that are vital to many species. Dormice inhabit the National Park, along with other increasingly rare mammals in the UK – brown hares, pine martens and red squirrels.

Paths, tracks and trails

The National Park is also a rich repository of Welsh culture, a land rich in myths and legends, where the Welsh language is widely spoken. It's a great place for getting out and about as it's laced with a seemingly endless number of walking and cycle routes: easy forest tracks, challenging mountain climbs, long-distance trails – there is something to suit everyone from families to fitness fanatics. Both walkers and cyclists can enjoy routes like the Mawddach Trail, a former railway line that runs for 9 miles (14km) between Dolgellau and Barmouth. Long-distance walks include the North Wales Path, a largely coastal trail stretching 60 miles (96km) from Prestatyn to Bangor, to the extremely challenging Cambrian Way (www.cambrianway.org.uk), which runs from Cardiff on the south coast, up through Snowdonia, over Snowdon and on to Conwy on the north coast. It's a lung-stretching 298 miles (479km) and not for the faint-hearted.

For more information on the Snowdonia National Park, check out www.snowdonia.gov.wales or go into one of the National Park Information Centres in Betws-y-coed, Beddgelert and Aberdyfi.

Mountain bike track in Coed-y-Brenin.

TOUR 8

Dolgellau to Cadair Idris and the Aran Mountains

This tour of around 40 miles (64km) brings you close to the mysterious peak of Cadair Idris and at a relaxed pace can take a whole day.

This tour starts at Dolgellau which, slightly offset from the great Bala-Tal-y-llyn geological fault line, stands near the southern entrance to the Snowdonia National Park. Apart from Cadair Idris, Snowdon's equivalent in the popularity stakes, less familiar country stretches southeast to the beautiful valley of the River Dyfi (often anglicised to Dovey). The vast Dyfi Forest, threaded by old slate-mining tracks, spreads its mantle of conifers over a complex, folded landscape. Some of the hilltops sport wind turbines, for this is 'alternative technology' territory. To the east of Dolgellau, the volcanic Aran mountains extend

Highlights
- Dolgellau
- Cadair Idris
- Centre for Alternative Technology
- Dinas Mawddwy
- Bwlch y Groes
- Coed-y-Brenin

from Dinas Mawddwy to Bala Lake, only failing by a whisker to reach the magic 3000ft (915m) but nevertheless boasting Wales's highest road. To the north lies the Coed-y-Brenin Forest, where larch and Sitka spruce clothe a hilly landscape whose streams all flow into the Mawddach;

Our Lady of Sorrows

On Meyrick Street in Dolgellau is Our Lady of Sorrows Church. It opened in the 1960s, thanks to a Maltese priest Francis Scalpell who had come here in 1939 and started to celebrate Mass in a former stable. With the help of Italian POWs he built a rudimentary church, but was determined to have a more permanent structure. Eventually he raised the necessary funds and this church is the result.

Father Scalpell contributed to the architect's design for the church.

it is an area of waterfalls, abandoned gold and copper mines and numerous forest trails, ideal for walkers and mountain bikers.

Dolgellau

The tour starts in **Dolgellau** ❶ which has for centuries provided hospitality for travellers and it remains a great favourite with visitors today. In the early 1400s, Owain Glyndwr assembled a parliament here, while in the nineteenth century it briefly became a hub of activity when gold was discovered in the surrounding rocks. However, the town's main significance revolved around its great sheep and cattle fairs and livestock are still brought in for the weekly market. The town's mostly nineteenth-century Market Square area of pale granite buildings is less bothered by traffic than it once was thanks to the road by-pass, but it is still a busy place. Narrow, irregular streets lined with shops and restaurants invite browsing, while to the north, not far from the parish church, St Mary's, with its medieval tower and excellent Victorian stained glass, a seven-arched bridge, **Bont Fawr**, spans the Afon Wnion.

The National Centre for Welsh Folk Music, **Ty Siamas** (www.tysiamas.

cymru/en/home), is located in a former market hall in the town centre. Live performances are staged here throughout the year, but the town's big event is July's Sesiwn Fawr, three days of exhilarating folk music, comedy and literature.

Dolgellau's buildings were constructed using local granite.

Cadair Idris

Follow the A470 east up to Cross Foxes and bear right onto the A487. High mountain country lies ahead, and from the pass (Bwlch Talyllyn) at 938ft (286m) there are stunning views down the crag-bound upper valley here on the Bala–Tal-y-llyn fault line (the largest land-shift in Wales) running northeast to southwest through southern Snowdonia. Tal-y-llyn Lake gleams in the distance, while up to the right rear the outlying flanks of **Cadair Idris** (Chair of Idris). This volcanic massif, eroded by aeons of glacial action into a peak of savage beauty, is named after Idris, a local hero killed in battle against the Saxons around AD 630. Tradition decrees that anyone sleeping overnight in the 'chair' (its precise position is unclear) will wake as either a lunatic or a poet.

You can park at **Minffordd ❷** to follow the **Minffordd Path** (6 miles/

Bont Fawr.

Corris' Railway Museum.

north shore provides an easy and pleasant walk to Minffordd.

Corris

The A487 Machynlleth road continues towards Corris, but most visitors first call at **Corris Craft Centre** (www.corriscraftcentre.co.uk) a purpose-built, modernist complex of studios in which crafts people can be observed making pottery, glass, leatherware, jewellery and candles, as well as chocolate and gin. There is also a restaurant and **King Arthur's Labyrinth** (www.kingarthurslabyrinth. co.uk; charge). Access is by boat through a magic waterfall to subterranean caverns where you then walk underground, while some of the Welsh legends pertaining to King Arthur are explored in tableaux with light and sound effects.

The town of **Corris** ❸, east off the main road, stands amidst the convoluted, timber-clad hills of Dyfi Forest. The village grew up around slate quarrying in the Afon Dulas valley, and a narrow-gauge railway was built in 1859 to transport slate down to the main line at Machynlleth. Steam locomotives replaced horses in 1879. For more details of this and the Corris Railway

9.6km return) for an ascent of Cadair Idris from the south. This route goes via the lovely Llyn Cau to Penygadair, 2929ft (893m), Cadair Idris's highest top, but although it's probably the shortest route up the mountain it's also the hardest, with an ascent of 2850ft (869m). It's a rough climb, as serious as Snowdon – but without trains or a café on top. Interestingly, during the late nineteenth century one Richard Pugh of Dolgellau did construct a stone hut on the summit in which he provided visitors with 'all convenient refreshments while waiting for the dispersion of the misty clouds in order to enjoy the exquisite prospect…' Pugh's hut remains, now downgraded to a basic shelter but welcome nonetheless. (For Cadair Idris from the north, see page 100.)

Less than a mile (1.3km) southwest of Minffordd on the B4405, cradled by sweeping mountainsides, stretch the waters of Tal-y-llyn Lake (or, to give it its true Welsh name, Llyn Mwyngil – Lake in the Pleasant Retreat). It is indeed a peaceful lake, shallow but abundant in fish and flora, notably its yellow water-lily. From the handsome Tyn y Cornel Hotel, and the adjacent little unspoilt church, a lakeside track along the

Cadair Idris.

Centre for Alternative Technology.

Society's restoration work, visit the **Railway Museum** (www.corris.co.uk; free). A 50-minute round trip on the train includes a guided tour of the sheds at Maespoeth Junction.

As well as a Heritage Trail north of the village, there are forest trails suitable for walking and cycling further up the Dulas valley around Aberllefenni.

Centre for Alternative Technology

Signed to the left off a bend in the descending A487 road is one of southern Snowdonia's most compelling visitor attractions. The **Centre for Alternative Technology** ❹ (Llwyngwern Quarry; www.cat.org.uk) was developed from modest beginnings in the early 1970s at a disused slate quarry near the hamlet of Pantperthog. Its ethos is to demonstrate the effectiveness of alternative energy sources, house insulation and organic food production.

By examining such technologies as solar, wind and wave power, house building and sustainable soil fertilisation, the centre challenges conventional views in a thought-provoking and entertaining way about how an advanced industrial society should utilise its resources. It would be easy to spend a whole day here, and it's a great attraction for all ages. Entry is by water-powered cliff railway, and within the 7 acres (2.8 hectares) can be found hands-on displays, organic gardens, a beehouse, a vegetarian café, a gift and bookshop and the excellent Quarry Trail. There is even an electric vehicle charge point for visitors arriving by electric car.

Dyfi Valley

Both the main A487 road and a parallel lane on the east bank of the Afon Dulas descend into the lovely **Dovey Valley** or **Dyffryn Dyfi**. Traditionally the frontier between north and south Wales, this is the modern-day meeting place of Gwynedd, Powys and Ceredigion. Across the Afon Dyfi stands Machynlleth, a colourful, bustling market town with many interesting features (see page 109).

Turn left on the B4404 past Llanwrin and stay on the northwest bank of the Dyfi on an unclassified road all the way to Aberangell and Minllyn, small villages on the eastern fringe of Dyfi Forest. On the skyline of Mynydd y Cemais to the southeast are ranged wind turbines belonging to the CAT's wind farm. The road closely shadows the dismantled Mawddwy Railway which, in the mid-nineteenth century, connected Dinas Mawddwy with the main Cambrian Railway at Cemmaes Road 7 miles (11km) to the south. Passenger services ceased in 1930 but the line was kept open for goods traffic until damage to a bridge over the Dyfi closed it more conclusively in 1951.

Ever industrious, the Victorians had planned to extend the Mawddwy line north to join the Great Western Railway at Llanuwchllyn (see page 46) by tunnelling beneath the Aran mountains. Unfortunately, the plan was never realised as the project's sponsor, local landowner Sir Edmund

Dyfi Forest and Valley.

Buckley, was declared bankrupt in 1876 before work began.

On the outskirts of Dinas Mawddwy on the A470 near Pont Minllyn, a seventeenth-century packhorse bridge, stands **Meirion Mill** (www.meirionmill.co.uk), a craft and clothing shop, plus a café, set in the old Dinas Mawddwy station buildings.

The Tudors

After Edward I's brutal conquest of Wales, there was a distinct irony in the fact that, in 1485 at the Battle of Bosworth, an English king (Richard III) was beaten by a Welshman, Henry Tudor, who gained the throne and became Henry VII. Henry ensured that Welshmen were rewarded with positions of power at court. However, his son, Henry VIII, put an end to Welsh independence by instituting the Acts of Union of 1536 and 1542. Although these gave the Welsh legal equality, they introduced English law to Wales and made English the language of the courts.

Henry Tudor was born in Pembroke Castle.

Dinas Mawddwy

Dinas Mawddwy ❺ itself was described by George Borrow in *Wild Wales* (published in 1862) as 'little more than a collection of filthy huts… Fierce-looking red-haired banditti of old were staggering about, and sounds of drunken revelry echoed from the huts…' Dinas, however, had once been a much more important place, with over 1000 inhabitants, shops, inns, several fairs and major cattle sales. Later prosperity came from lead mining and slate quarrying. Today the village, snug in an amphitheatre of wooded and rhododendron-clad hills at the confluence of the Dyfi and Cerist rivers, enjoys a more peaceful existence as a walking centre.

A head for heights is needed
for the Precipice Walk.

Bwlch y Groes

To the north lie the volcanic Aran Mountains, which extend to Bala Lake and culminate in Aran Fawddwy (2969ft/905m). To explore the Aran ridge, drive northeast to Aber-Cywarch and there turn left to Cwm Cywarch. Following access problems in the 1980s, the Arans are regaining their popularity, but keep to the concessionary paths and heed the 'No Dogs' signs. Being properly equipped and choosing favourable weather become even more vital in remote hills such as these. As a detour to the route, the unclassified mountain road continues beside the Afon Dyfi to Llanymawddwy, shortly beyond which the river is crossed and the scenery grows appreciably wilder by

Dinas Mawddwy.

Bwlch y Groes, or Hellfire Pass.

the minute. Precipitous slopes up to 1000ft (300m) high, deeply scarred by stream beds, crowd in ahead. The road is correspondingly steep as it climbs the tributary valley of the Afon Rhiwlech, passes a right fork to Lake Vyrnwy and reaches **Bwlch y Groes**, 1788ft (545m) above sea level. There is car parking here at Wales's highest road pass and views extend north towards the Arenig mountains and west to the Arans – a truly spectacular spot to be attained by vehicle. The road descends to Llanuwchllyn, not far from the southern end of Bala Lake (see page 84), from where you can join the A494 back to Dolgellau.

The Torrent Walk and Precipice Walk

A direct return to Dolgellau from Dinas Mawddwy can be made on the A470. Ascending the Cerist valley to Bwlch Oerddrws (Cold Door Pass) at 1178ft (359m), it skirts scenic cwms and waterfalls. Beyond the pass there are magnificent views of Cadair Idris.

After passing Cross Foxes once again, about 2.5 miles (4km) before reaching Dolgellau, turn sharp right onto the B4416 to **Brithdir ❻**. Half a mile (0.8km) before the village, a path opposite St Mark's Church marks the start of the popular **Torrent Walk**. About 2.5 miles (4km) in length, the path's best stretch drops through beautiful deciduous woodland beside a series of waterfalls in the fast-flowing Afon Clywedog.

Continue on the B4416 to Bont Newydd, cross the junction with the A494, and follow the narrow, twisting lane to the tiny settlement of Llanfachreth. (There is a wider, unclassified road that reaches here from Dolgellau via the slopes of Foel Offrwm.)

The best-known **Precipice Walk**, and the first to be established in the Snowdonia region, begins southwest of Llanfachreth from roadside car parking (Saithgroesffordd), where the road forks for Ty'n Groes. Much of the 3-mile (5km) circular walk, which takes in lovely Llyn Cynwch and stunning views over the Mawddach estuary, is an easy and intrinsically safe route. In places, however, it does traverse very

Coed-y-Brenin.

steep hillside. The path is not a public right of way; instead, it has enjoyed a concessionary status since 1890, courtesy of the Nannau Estate.

Coed-y-Brenin

Llanfachreth nestles at the southern edge of the magnificent **Coed-y-Brenin** (The King's Forest), so named after George V's Silver Jubilee in 1935. Despite impressive commercial statistics (yielding thousands of tons of timber annually), Coed-y-Brenin remains one of the most varied and lovely forests in Wales. Situated in what used to be Meirioneth, it straddles the rivers Gamlan, Eden, Gain and Wen, along with the Mawddach into which all the others flow. Within the forest can be found wooded gorges, crags, waterfalls and boulder-strewn rivers, secluded upland pastures and a scattering of farmsteads.

Stunning views can be enjoyed from the café and restaurant at the **Coed-y-Brenin Visitor Centre** ❼ (tel: 01341 440747). Situated to the east of the A470, 8 miles (13km) north of Dolgellau, the Centre also has cycle hire, showers and a children's adventure playground. Pick up details of the many waymarked walking and mountain-biking forest trails; it is possible to plan delightful rambles or mountain-bike tours from any of the numerous car parks and picnic areas.

Glasdir

At **Glasdir** ❽ less than a mile (1.6km) west of Llanfachreth on the banks of the tumbling Afon Las, an arboretum of mountain tree species has been established. Further down still are the ruins of **Glasdir Copper Mine**, which you can explore on a short walking trail from Glasdir. The copper mine opened in 1852; however, the mineral had probably been extracted since prehistoric times. At the height of its activity, Glasdir Mine produced 50 tons of ore per day. The mine finally closed in 1914.

From Glasdir take the left-hand of two parallel lanes dropping to the Afon Wen and cross the river near its confluence with the Afon Eden. In under a mile (1.6km) this forestry by road crosses the Afon Eden and joins the A470. Ahead at Ganllwyd there is car parking for a short walk west up to Rhaeadr Du and a sequence of beautiful waterfalls in the Afon Gamlan.

Waterfalls

At the end of the adopted road beside the infant Afon Mawddach northeast from Ganllwyd (to the east of the A470), a rough track continues to Bont Gwynfynydd. Here the rivers Mawddach and Gain each roar over their own spectacular **waterfalls** – Rhaeadr Mawddach and Pistyll Gain –

before joining forces near the site of the old Gwynfynydd Gold Mine. Stocks of the metal have now disappeared – it is so rare it fetches three times the price of ordinary gold. Pure Welsh gold bears the 'Welsh Maiden' mark and the hallmark 'Aur Cymru'.

Parallel to the A470 for some distance to the east, lies the course of Sarn Helen, an ancient north-to-south Roman road (though most went east towards Offa's Dyke). It was adapted by the Romans for their own use to link Caerhun, near Conwy (see page 21), with Maridunum (Carmarthen) and can still be traced, intermittently, throughout the entire length of Wales. According to the Mabinogion, a collection of mythical stories dating back to the thirteenth century, the road was laid in the fourth century AD by Helen, noble bride of the self-styled Emperor Magnus Maximus who was dream-led to Wales by his vision of her.

Eating Out

DOLGELLAU

Royal Ship

Queen's Square; www.royalship.pub. This hotel restaurant, in a fine old stone building in Dolgellau, offers above average pub mains like banana blossom chilli bites, and meatball penang curry, a regularly changing menu of modern British dishes, with plenty of Welsh produce. Lamb rump, fish and beef feature frequently, and there are always vegetarian options. Try the Penderyn Welsh whisky and honey ice cream for dessert. Otherwise, it's a lovely spot to sup on a pint whilst watching the world (well, Dolgellau) go by. ££

T.H. Roberts

Parliament House, Bridge Street; tel: 01341 423552; closed Sun.
Starting with the fabulous full breakfasts, this café, in a former ironmonger shop, serves the most delectable home-made cakes, light lunches and probably the best coffee in town. It has a lovely old-world ambience with books and papers to read while you relax. £

NR LLANELLTYD

The Brigands Inn

Mallwyd; www.brigandsinn.com.
This restored fifteenth-century coaching inn serves breakfast, lunch and dinner, as well as light meals in the afternoons. Choose from home-made ciabatta rolls, gluten-free bagels and steaks. Or join them for Sunday lunch. Desserts are home-made and delicious. ££

The Eagles Inn

Llanuwchllyn; www.yr-eagles.co.uk; closed Mon & Tues.
This pub in the little village of Llanuwchllyn serves real ales and a good selection of dishes, using local produce, much of which comes from the family farm. There are several vegetarian options, such as home-made vegetable lasagne, and a children's menu. Check out the great range of desserts, including home-made bread and butter pudding. £

Mawddach

Llanelltyd, by the A470 outside Dolgellau; www.mawddach.com; closed Sun–Wed.
This sleek, contemporary barn conversion offers views of Cadair Idris and the Mawddach estuary. Located on the family farm and run by two brothers, the dinner menu focuses on stone-baked Neapolitan pizzas: the aubergine parmigiana or spicy nduja are particularly decent. Still hungry? Snack on deep-fried arancini balls. ££

Hiking in the Cadair
Idris mountain range.

TOUR 9

Cadair Idris to Machynlleth

This 48-mile (77km) full-day tour takes you past the
peaks of Cadair Idris, then along the Cardigan Coast, before
heading back inland to the ancient town of Machynlleth.

Between the Mawddach and the Dyfi
(Dovey) estuaries lies a bulge of high
land rising to Cadair Idris and split
through the middle by the Bala–
Talyllyn geological fault. Mountain
roads probe the heart of this, the
Snowdonia National Park's most
southerly outpost with its ancient
churches, castle ruins, 'Great Little
Trains' and links with the legend of
King Arthur. At Fairbourne, Tywyn
and Aberdyfi, long sandy beaches
provide the setting for holiday
activities without the razzmatazz of
more commercially developed resorts.
With the southern flanks of Cadair
Idris examined in Tour 8 (see page
92), this route sees what the great
mountain has to offer from the north
and east, alternating between coast

and foothills to arrive, ultimately,
at Machynlleth, the southernmost
gateway to Snowdonia and a town
with a rich Welsh history.

Cadair Idris

This route starts in **Dolgellau** ❶
(see page 91). Many come to
this attractive town to explore the

> **Highlights**
> - Cadair Idris
> - Cregennen Lakes
> - Fairbourne Steam Railway
> - Castell y Bere
> - Talyllyn Railway
> - Aberdyfi
> - Machynlleth

landscape around **Cadair Idris**, the mountain range whose craggy northern escarpment dominates the horizon. Some come to climb its peaks, though it can be rough walking. Already by the mid-eighteenth century, guides were leading visitors to the 2927ft (893m) summit of Penygadair, the highest peak on the Cadair Idris range. Nowadays so many tramp up the mountain that footpath erosion is causing serious problems.

Fork left up the old coaching road, a narrow lane which leaves Dolgellau from the west end of Fford Cader Idris (Cadair Idris Street), and in 1 mile (1.6km) turn right to pass roadside Llyn Gwernan. The well-known **Fox's Path** up Cadair Idris starts here, but is now so badly eroded that it is no longer recommended. Further

Footpath around Cregennen Lakes.

on at the Ty Nant car park at Pont Dyffrydan is the official start of the Pony Path over to Cwm Pennant; from the saddle at its highest point (Rhiw

Traditional steam trains at Fairbourne Steam Railway, Arthog.

Gwredydd), Cadair Idris's highest peak, Penygadair, is easily reached.

Cregennen lakes

The road meanders along beneath frowning cliffs rising almost 1500ft (450m) to Craig-las. About 300yds/m after crossing a cattle grid, turn off right to enjoy the two idyllically situated **Cregennen lakes** (Llynau Cregennen), which are popular with trout fishermen. They occupy part of a 705-acre (285-hectare) National Trust property donated in 1959 by Major C.L. Wynne-Jones in memory of his two sons killed in World War II. Standing stones marked on the Ordnance Survey map date from around 1800 BC; as with others in Snowdonia their exact purpose is unknown, but they might have been deity symbols, or boundary or route markers. The heights of Cadair Idris loom to the east, with the Mawddach estuary stretching below to the west: glorious views of both can be had from the summit of the easily climbed hill immediately to the north of the lakes. The name 'Cregennen' is said to derive from 'crog-gangen', which means 'hanging branch'. Criminals were often hung from an oak tree in this area.

Arthog

A tortuous descent ensues to reach **Arthog ❷**. Waterfalls punctuate the stream flowing down through

Cregennen Lakes.

Arthur and Merlin receive Excalibur
from the Lady of the Lake.

King Arthur

Was King Arthur a Welshman? Many people think so and claim that his last battle was fought at Camlan in Snowdonia. Others think it was fought on Snowdon itself and that Llyn Llydaw, a lake at the foot of the mountain, was the stretch of water across which the dying king was rowed to reach the island of Avalon. In Welsh, his name, Arth Fawr, means the Great Bear, and some think he was a Celtic god. Others consider it more likely that he was a fifth-century Celtic chieftain who fought against the Saxons.

the village; few would guess that it rises in the tiniest of glacial corrie lakes – Llyn Cyri – high under Cadair Idris's outlying crags. Passing near Arthog, a 9-mile (15km) -long nature trail, established by the RSPB and the North Wales Naturalists' Trust, utilises the trackbed of the old Aberystwyth and Welsh Coast Railway (1865–1965). Called the **Mawddach Trail** (see page 76), it skirts the estuary's very shoreline and is suitable for walking or cycling. The route runs between Dolgellau and Barmouth. There is also a **circular walk** of 9 miles (14km) from Arthog that takes you into the hills. It runs through woodland that is a Site of Special Scientific Interest (SSSI), which has stunning displays of bluebells in spring, and goes past a 200-year-old beech tree and the remains of a twelfth-century courtroom.

From Arthog, the road runs to **Fairbourne**, a settlement of mostly modern bungalows, which is home to the fascinating **Fairbourne Steam Railway** ❸ (www.fairbournerailway. com; check timetable for details). The railway runs for two miles (3.2km)

out along a duney sandspit to Penrhyn Point. Dating back to 1895 and horse-drawn until 1916, the railway was originally a narrow-gauge conveyance of building materials. From the route, glorious river and mountain views can be enjoyed and there is a seasonal foot-passenger ferry across to Barmouth (see page 75). An alternative crossing of the estuary can be made on

Cyclists on the Mawddach Trail.

Walks up Cadair Idris

There are three maintained routes up Cadair Idris. The toughest is the Minffordd Path, which starts from Dol Idris car park after the junction of the A487 and B4405 Dolgellau to Tywyn road. It's a 6-mile (9.7km) return route. The Pony Path, which is a similar distance, starts from the car park at Ty Nant farm, and is the classic ascent offering the best views. The Llanfihangel-y-pennant Path is the longest route at 10 miles (16km) return, but the easiest walk. It starts in Llanfihangel-y-pennant.

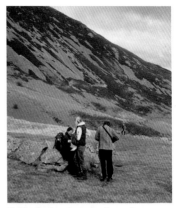

Walking boots, water and waterproof clothing are essential.

the Cambrian Coast railway viaduct which has a pedestrian walkway (see page 65).

Llwyngwril

One and three-quarter miles (3km) beyond **Llwyngwril** on the A493 coast road, adjacent to a railway halt, stands **Llangelynnin Church**. Set just above the shingle beach, this primitive, mainly twelfth-century building is dedicated to a local seventh-century saint, Celynnin, and sits on the site of a much earlier structure. The church features some wall paintings, including the Ten Commandments written in Welsh, and medieval gravestones inscribed in both Welsh and English can be found in the graveyard. Near the church is a Holy Well, the waters of which were once thought to heal sick children.

Llanegryn Church

Heading south, high coastal hills force the A493 inland although the railway manages to squeeze past. In less than 2 miles (3km) bear left to **Llanegryn**, notable for another little church. This one sits on a hillside half a mile (800m) northwest of the village and

reveals a remarkably beautiful rood screen and loft, probably carved by local craftsmen in the fifteenth or early sixteenth centuries, or, as tradition has it, brought there from Cymer Abbey near Dolgellau (see page 91) during the Reformation.

Castell y Bere

The Afon Dysynni is crossed opposite the dramatic, soaring buttress of Craig yr Aderyn (Birds' Rock), the only inland cormorant nesting site in Britain. Straight over the crossroads, in a wild and romantic setting at the heart of mountainous country and with fabulous views of the western flanks of Cadair Idris, stand the extensive but fragmentary ruins of **Castell y Bere** ❹ (www.cadw. gov.wales/visit/places-to-visit/ castell-y-bere; free), an example of a native Welsh (rather than Norman or Edwardian) castle. Started by Llewellyn the Great around 1221, the fortress guarded southern Meirionydd and the mountain route to Dolgellau. During the early part of 1283 Castell y Bere became one of Prince Dafydd ap Gruffydd's final refuges but was eventually surrendered later that

The Talyllyn Railway train.

same year to Edward I's 3000-strong invading army. It was the last Welsh castle to fall, and although it was briefly re-taken, it was eventually destroyed and left to the elements.

Llanfihangel-y-Pennant

At the road's end beyond **Llanfihangel-y-pennant**, a monument to Mary Jones has been installed in the ruin of her cottage, Tyn-y-ddol. In 1800, aged only 16, she walked barefoot over to Bala (about 26 miles/42km) to buy a Welsh Bible from the Methodist minister there, Thomas Charles (see page 84). He had none to sell but gave her his own. Mary's zeal for the scriptures so impressed him that he began a campaign, from which grew the British and Foreign Bible Society. From the adjacent road-end you can join the Pony Path for the classic ascent over the shoulder of Cadair Idris and on to Dolgellau.

Talyllyn Railway

Return to the crossroads and bear left to **Abergynolwyn**. Once an important slate quarrying centre, the village nestles in the Dysynni valley surrounded by forestry. Here, short of Tal-y-llyn Lake itself, stands Nant Gwernol Station (forest walks but no road access), northern terminus of the famous 2ft 3in (68cm) narrow-gauge **Talyllyn Railway** ❺ (www.talyllyn. co.uk). The line is the oldest of its kind in the world and one of the best known of Wales's 'Great Little Trains'. In continuous service since 1865, originally used to transport slate to the main line at Tywyn down on the coast, its trains now merrily puff the 7.25 miles (11.6km) between Nant

The ruins of Castell y Bere.

Aberdyfi.

Gwernol and Tywyn with cargoes of sightseers. The line was saved from obscurity in 1951 by the Tal-y-llyn Railway Preservation Society, the world's first such organisation, which has since been emulated by many similar groups. The entire railway journey of an hour each way can be varied by alighting at intermediate stations. A short walk from Dolgoch Station, for example, leads through woods to the attractive **Dolgoch Falls**; below the falls the line is carried across the little gorge on an impressive viaduct. There are also forest walks in the Nant Gwernol ravine.

Tywyn

Running parallel to the railway, the B4405 meets the A493 at Bryncrug, 2 miles (3km) from **Tywyn ⑥**. This is where the railway's main station is situated, together with the **Narrow Gauge Railway Museum** (www.narrowgaugerailwaymuseum. org.uk; free but donations welcome), which combines displays of old locomotives with the history of the slate mining industry in North and

Mid Wales. The museum has a section devoted to the Rev. W.V. Awdry, the creator of Thomas the Tank Engine. Rev Awdry was once a volunteer on the Talyllyn Railway. **Tywyn's** evolution as a seaside resort owed much to John Corbett, a salt baron from Droitwich who built Marine Terrace, the Market Hall and the Assembly Rooms (now a cinema). Adjacent to the latter stands St

Aberdyfi pier.

The Owain Glyndwr Centre in Machynlleth.

Cadfan's Church, in which will be found the seventh-century St Cadfan's Stone bearing an inscription thought to be the oldest example of written Welsh in existence.

Aberdyfi

Dunes seaward of the road and railway extend south to **Aberdyfi** ❼ (Aberdovey – meaning 'Mouth of the Dovey'), a pleasant resort best known for its golf course and sailing facilities. The Tourist Information Centre on The Wharf (www.aberdyfi-council. wales/aberdovey-tourist-information-centre) provides an accommodation booking service, guide books and maps of local walks. Aberdyfi boasts a major Outward Bound Centre and is popular with windsurfers, kitesurfers and sailors. Aberdyfi is also the starting point for the 108-mile (174km) **Dyfi Valley Way** exploring countryside on both flanks of the river north to its source under Aran Fawddwy, and crossing the site of King Arthur's legendary last battle at Camlan. The Dyfi is the traditional frontier between North and South

Wales. The **Meirionnydd Coast Walk** also starts at Aberdyfi, the route passing standing stones and holy wells as it takes you along the coast to Porthmadog. The path is 72 miles (116km) long and can be split into eight easy one-day sections.

Aberdyfi's profile was raised when Charles Dibdin composed the song *The Bells of Aberdovey* for his opera *Liberty Hall* in 1785. Of many stories surrounding the mysteriously pealing bells beneath the sea, the most commonly quoted (and embellished) concerns Cantre'r Gwaelod – the Lowland Hundred. This once fertile low-lying plain was protected from the sea by dykes in the care of Seithennin, a notorious drunkard. One stormy night, while making merry at a feast, he forgot to close the sluices. The Lowland Hundred was inundated and Manua, its principal settlement containing the bells,

Owain Glyndwr

Owain Glyndwr (c.1350–1416) is a name you will hear wherever you travel in North Wales. Descended from the Princes of Powys, Glyndwr was wealthy and educated, and even served in the English army. When a nobleman in Ruthin appropriated some of his land, Glyndwr appealed to the courts but lost his case: the nobleman was close to Henry IV. Glyndwr gathered supporters and attacked Ruthin, the start of a rebellion against English rule. He took castles, including Harlech, and proclaimed the first Welsh parliament in Machynlleth in 1404. However, by 1408 when Harlech was taken by royal forces, he was forced into hiding somewhere in Snowdonia and vanished into obscurity. No one even knows where he is buried.

Machynlleth

At Pen-y-bont turn right over the river and beneath the railway line to enter **Machynlleth ❾**. The town's centrepiece is a splendid Victorian Clock Tower built in 1873 to commemorate the Marquess of Londonderry's family who then owned the imposing seventeenth-century Plas Machynlleth, set in parkland to the south.

One of the town's most historic sites is the late medieval **Owain Glyndwr Centre** (www.canolfanowainglyndwr.org; free) in the Parliament House. This building incorporates the remains of an earlier structure in which the Welsh people's hero established the country's first Parliament in 1404. George Borrow lodged at the town-centre Wynstay Hotel during his tour of Wales in 1854.

The **Museum of Modern Art** (MOMA) is in The Tabernacle, a former Wesleyan Chapel (www.moma.cymru; free). The museum has a permanent collection of contemporary artworks, primarily from artists living or working in Wales. There are also temporary exhibitions and concerts.

Ynys-hir Nature Reserve

This route ends here but travel just a few miles south-west of Machynlleth to **Ynys-hir Nature Reserve** (www.rspb.org.uk). This extensive reserve provides a home for a wide range of birds such as egrets, redshanks and wood warblers. There are five hides, two viewpoints and two circular nature trails, making it a great place for the whole family.

Eating Out

NR DOLGELLAU

Penmaenuchaf Hall

Penmaenpool (1.5 miles/2.4km west of Dolgellau); www.penmaenuchaf.co.uk. Elegant dining in the garden restaurant of this country hotel combines contemporary features such as Welsh slate floors with white tablecloths and candlelight. A modern British menu features dishes such as curried swede with charred onion, and Rhug Estate organic Welsh lamb. £££

ABERDYFI

Penhelig Arms

Terrace Road; www.penheligarmspubaberdyfi.co.uk. This seafront hotel offers well-loved classics such as Sunday roasts and sausage and mash. There are also sandwiches, jacket potatoes and two-course set menus (Mon–Fri) on offer. Vegetarian choices also feature. ££

MACHYNLLETH

Tŷ Medi

Heol Maengwyn; www.ty-medi.co.uk. Formely the *Quarry Café*, this vegetarian and vegan restaurant serves omelettes, loaded burgers and pastries across their brunch, lunch and afternoon treats menus. Gluten-free options also available. £

NR MACHYNLLETH

Ynyshir Hall

Eglwysfach (off A487); www.ynyshir.co.uk. This fabulous restaurant holds two Michelin star and is a serious dining experience, albeit at an eye-watering price. Dishes are meat-focused with a few fish options. Attention to detail is paramount, as is the provenance of the food, which is served as a series of small integrated dishes. £££

Walkers ascending Snowdon.

TRIP TIPS
Active Pursuits

North Wales, and the Snowdonia National Park in particular, is a marvellous place for getting active. The wild landscape offers rigorous challenges as well as gentle exercise – and whether you're super-fit or a family wanting some fun in the fresh air, there's something to suit you. By far the most popular outdoor pursuit is walking, closely followed by mountain biking and climbing. But you can also enjoy pony trekking, canoeing and kayaking, and even golf.

Walking

There's an almost bewildering choice of walking routes, ranging from long-distance waymarked paths to forest tracks and nature trails. There are, however, plenty of guidebooks and leaflets available at information centres and bookshops. Climbing Snowdon or Cadair Idris are popular goals but their often-congested paths are not to everyone's taste – and they're obviously not for novices. Each mountain range enjoys its own distinctive character. In the north the Carneddau offer vast grassy whaleback ridges, while the adjacent Glyders and Tryfan are strewn with frost-shattered boulders. Behind Tremadog Bay rise the Rhinogs, unfrequented mountains of ankle-twisting rock and deep heather. Both the Cadair Idris and Snowdon massifs offer rugged walking, sustained gradients and wonderful views.

By contrast, the featureless and often boggy Migneint between Bala and Ffestiniog is strictly for connoisseurs of solitude. The Aran ridge running north from Dinas Mawddwy to Bala Lake is regaining popularity after access problems. West and north of Blaenau Ffestiniog, the Moelwyns are laced with the fascinating relics of slate mining.

Get golfing

The North Wales coast is home to some excellent golf courses. The finest is Royal St David's Golf Club in Harlech (www.royalstdavids.co.uk), a championship links course that sits beneath Harlech Castle. There are also courses on the Lleyn Peninsula at Abersoch, Nefyn and Pwllheli; a course at Porthmadog and one further down the coast at Aberdyfi – for information see www.golfnorthwales.co.uk.

For family groups and the less mobile there are miles of gentler footpaths and bridleways to explore. Good examples may be found in Gwydir Forest around Betws-y-Coed, in Coed-y-Brenin Forest near Dolgellau and around many of Snowdonia's more accessible lakes. The 4-mile Great Orme circular walk (6.5km) is a nature trail for all the family. A coastal path of 125 miles (200km) has been developed around the shoreline of Anglesey, and a 91-mile (146km) path snakes around the edge of the Lleyn Peninsula. Waymarked long-distance trails include the 108-mile (174km) Dyfi Valley Way and the 60-mile (97km) North Wales Path between Prestatyn and Bangor (for information on trails, visit www.visitwales.com/things-do/adventure-and-activities/walking).

Of various challenge walks, the most famous is the Welsh 3000s (www.welsh3000s.co.uk), a gruelling 30-mile (48km) tramp over all 15 of Snowdonia's 3000ft (914m) -plus summits within a 24-hour period. For ultra runners, however, the ultimate challenge is the Dragon's Back Race, an epic 380-km, six-day trail beginning at Conwy Castle and ending at Cardiff Castle; the majority of starters do not finish.

National Park walks

Details of mountain and leisure walks in Snowdonia National Park appear on the official website: www.snowdonia.gov.wales, together with details of special events. Some walks also appear in the free visitor magazine *Eryri*. Routes are graded for difficulty and duration. It's important to be properly shod and clothed for walking. Even on low-level paths the weather can change quickly, while on the tops, protection from the elements may become vital for survival. Since the installation of an automatic, solar-powered weather station on Snowdon's summit, with hourly data relayed to base stations by mobile phone, reliable mountain forecasts are now assured (tel: 0370 900 0100; www.metoffice.gov.uk).

Climbing

Snowdonia's great buttresses and gullies have attracted rock climbers in ever greater numbers since before World War I when Colin Kirkus and John Menlove Edwards pioneered

The golf course at Nefyn, along the Lleyn Peninsula.

audacious new ascents. Later, in the 1950s, the likes of Joe Brown and Don Whillans immortalised such locations as the Llanberis Pass and Snowdon's Clogwyn Du'r Arddu. More recently, interest has spread out from the inland crags to embrace the sea cliffs of Anglesey, the Lleyn Peninsula, Llandudno's Great Orme and the cliffs north of Tremadog. While it is feasible for confident hillwalkers to tackle scrambling routes (requiring the use of hands as well as feet), climbing with ropes should only be attempted by experienced climbers. Courses in hillwalking, climbing, mountaineering and associated sports, including canoeing and kayaking, are provided at Wales's National Mountain Sports Centre at Plas-y-Brenin, Capel Curig (www.pyb.co.uk).

Mountain biking

Every kind of cycling terrain exists in the Snowdonia region, from meandering back-lanes to severe mountain gradients. Off-road riding is permitted on public bridleways, unclassified roads and on specially waymarked cycle tracks such as those in the Gwydir and Coed-y-Brenin forests. Cycling is not permitted on footpaths or over trackless countryside. Under the Snowdon Voluntary Cycling Agreement, cyclists are requested not to ride up to, or down from, the summit of Snowdon between 10am and 5pm from 1 May to 30 September. There is full access from October to the end of April. A leaflet available at cycle shops, warden centres and tourist information centres outlines alternative routes through mountainous terrain in the Snowdon area. With careful use of an OS map, many worthwhile itineraries 'off the beaten track' can be devised to suit individual abilities, from beginners to experts. The gentle countryside and quiet country lanes of Anglesey and the Lleyn Peninsula make them ideal for family cycling; an ideal family day out! Bike hire outlets include: Dolgellau Cycles (The Old Furnace, Smithfield Street, Dolgellau; www.dolgellaucycles.co.uk); Beics Brenin (Coed-y-Brenin Visitor Centre, Dollgellau; www.beicsbrenin. co.uk); 1085 Adventures (The Bike Barn, Beddgelert Forest; www.1085 adventures.co.uk).

Horse-trekking through Gwydir Forest.

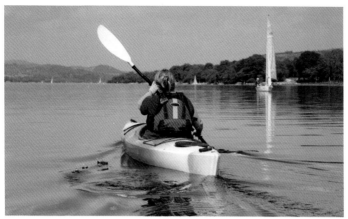

Canoeing on Lake Bala.

Horse riding

You do not have to be an expert to enjoy pony trekking. Trekking centres will match horses to individual riding ability; the pace is relaxed and younger children can go along too. Riding and hacking are for the more experienced, with trail riding, sometimes over several days, the most adventurous option. Welsh mountain ponies and the smaller Welsh cobs are used at most riding/trekking centres. Access to the countryside is virtually the same as for mountain biking. Regional centres include Snowdonia Riding Stables at Waunfawr, near Caernarfon (www.snowdoniaridingstables.co.uk) and the Isle of Anglesey Riding Centre at Tal-y-foel farm, near Dwyran on Anglesy (www.tal-y-foel. co.uk). Visit the Wales Trekking and Riding Association website for further information: www.ridingwales.com.

Water sports

Snowdonia's long coastline bordering Cardigan Bay and the Irish Sea is a premier venue for dinghy sailing. There are excellent marinas at Conwy, Caernarfon and Pwllheli, as well as numerous sheltered moorings in fishing harbours and bays. Surfing, windsurfing and sea-kayaking are catered for by a coast offering exposure to, or protection from, all points of the compass. For more information contact the National Outdoor Centre (www.plasmenai.co.uk) at Plas Menai.

Inland, canoeing is enjoyed on mountain lakes and challenging rivers, while paddleboarding has become a hugely popular lake-bound pursuit; Llyn Gwynant is superb for this. For suitable locations and prevailing conditions contact the National White Water Centre near Bala (www.nationalwhitewatercentre.co.uk).

Downhill adventure

The Llandudno Snowsports Centre (www.jnlllandudno.co.uk) is a great place for kids to let off steam – and adults too. There's a dry ski slope, where you can have a go at both skiing and snowboarding (children must be over 4 years of age), as well as a toboggan run which is (2460ft) 750m long. The centre also has Sno-tubes: inflatable rings which you climb into then ride downhill at high speed.

Themed Holidays

There's plenty of potential for themed breaks in North Wales and the Snowdonia National Park – and there are opportunities for both adults and children. Most options involve exploring the outdoors in some way, but there are more sedate breaks on offer too. The options below will give you some ideas.

Art

The lush landscape of North Wales makes it an ideal spot for painting holidays. HF Holidays (tel: 020 3974 8865 for bookings; www.hfholidays. co.uk) offer a 7-day Landscape Painting at Dolgellau course, where an accomplished artist caters for all levels of experience. There's also the Bodnant Art Studio (www.bodnantart.com), where Paul Pigram offers various paint and pastel workshops.

Conservation

Snowdonia is so popular with walkers and cyclists that footpath erosion is a serious problem. So the National Trust often runs working holidays in the area, in which volunteers help to fix footpaths on the mountains. They also run breaks in which volunteers help control invasive species in the countryside – plants like Japanese knotweed and Himalayan balsam. The type of activity varies annually. For information www.nationaltrust.org.uk.

Cookery

If you want to brush up on your cooking skills while you're on holiday in Wales, then you could sign up for a course at the Bodnant Welsh Food Cookery School in Conwy (www.bodnant-welshfood.co.uk), where you can learn how to make both Welsh specialities and global cuisines using local ingredients.

Outdoor adventure

The Plas-y-Brenin National Mountain Sports Centre in Capel Curig (www.pyb.co.uk) is at the heart of the Snowdonia National Park and offers a wide range of residential courses in everything from rock climbing and hillwalking to canoeing. Courses cater for a range of abilities: there are courses for those who wish to become a mountain or hill leader, as well as ones for families who want an introduction to kayaking.

The National White Water Centre, near Bala (www.national whitewatercentre.co.uk), offers short courses with accommodation, in which you combine white-water rafting with another activity such as canyoning, rock climbing, mountain biking or clay pigeon shooting. There's also a bushcraft course that teaches you all the essential skills of survival, such as shelter building and water sourcing.

Learn to climb at the National Mountain Sports Centre, Plas-y-Brenin.

Tackling the River Tryweryn at the National White Water Centre.

Railway breaks

Steam railway fans might want to join one of the driver experience courses run by some of the famous vintage railways in North Wales, offering the opportunity to get 'hands-on' with a real steam locomotive. The Llangollen Railway (www.llangollen-railway.co.uk), Fairbourne Railway (www.fairbournerailway.com), and Talyllyn Railway (www.talyllyn.co.uk) all offer driver experience days.

Retreats

If you're after some inner peace and love the calm of the countryside, then you might want to join one of the many retreats held at St Bueno's Spirituality Centre, near St Asaph (www.beunos.com). This former Jesuit college was where poet Gerard Manley Hopkins trained for the priesthood, and where he was inspired to write many of his poems. As well as weekend and week-long retreats, St Beuno's also runs a variety of spirituality courses.

Welsh language

The Welsh language is an ancient Celtic tongue, most closely related to Cornish and Breton (see page 60). It is still widely spoken in North Wales and you can get to grips with its lyrical sounds on an intensive residential course at the Welsh Language Centre, Nant Gwrtheyrn (www.nantgwrtheyrn.org), on the Lleyn Peninsula. Courses are available for complete beginners, as well as those with some knowledge of the language.

The Talyllyn Railway.

Practical Information

Here you'll find all the essential practical information you need to make your trip to Snowdonia and North Wales run smoothly.

Getting there

By road

Access from the northwest is now excellent thanks to the A55 North Wales Expressway which continues beneath the Conwy Estuary to Bangor and Holyhead. For the Vale of Conwy, Betws-y-coed and the Vale of Ffestiniog, take the southbound A470 from Glan Conwy. Thomas Telford's London to Holyhead highway, now the A5, heads west from the M54 via Llangollen to Capel Curig and thence through the mountains to Bethesda and the A55.

Befitting its Roman origins, Caernarfon sits at the hub of radiating roads. The A4085 and A4086 flank Snowdon itself, while the A497/499 strikes southwest for the Lleyn Peninsula. Two parallel north-south roads link the Vale of Ffestiniog with the River Mawddach, taking in the Cardigan Bay resorts and Coed-y-brenin forest.

Southwest from Bala towards Dolgellau the A494 follows a major geological fault line. Southeastern Snowdonia is approached on the A470 from Llanidloes and Newtown, or the A458 from Shrewsbury.

By coach

National Express operate services from London and Manchester to Aberystwyth, Bangor, Holyhead and Llandudno (www.nationalexpress.com). Arriva provide services throughout Wales to Bangor, Caernarfon, Colwyn Bay, Llandudno, Porthmadog and Wrexham (www.arrivabus.co.uk).

By train

Train services from London Euston run to Chester or Crewe, where passengers can change for Holyhead, with stops at Llandudno Junction and Bangor. Other local trains call at Conwy, Penmaenmawr, Llanfairfechan and stations on Anglesey. Blaenau Ffestiniog is reached by a branch line through the Vale of Conwy from Llandudno Junction. From Blaenau Ffestiniog the narrow-gauge Ffestiniog Railway runs down to Porthmadog, connecting at Minffordd station with the scenic Cambrian Coast Line between Pwllheli and Aberystwyth. Services to and from the Midlands via Shrewsbury connect to Machynlleth.

The B4391, the old pre-power station road from Porthmadog to Bala, strikes out across the Migneint.

The Sherpa buses reduce congestion in the National Park.

For all timetable and fare enquiries, www.nationalrail.co.uk.

By plane

The nearest international airports to North Wales are Manchester (www.manchesterairport.co.uk), Liverpool (www.liverpoolairport.com) and Birmingham (www.birmingham airport.co.uk). Cardiff Airport (www.cardiff-airport.com) has links to airports in Ireland and Scotland, as well as various European destinations.

By ferry

There are ferry services, including a high-speed, car-carrying catamaran, between Ireland and Wales: Dublin is linked to Holyhead on Anglesey, and there are also services between Rosslare and Fishguard, in South Wales. Stena Line, www.stenaline.co.uk; Irish Ferries, www.irishferries.com.

Getting around

Public transport

For local bus journeys enquire at a TIC. The Explore Wales Pass gives four days' train and bus travel within an eight-day period, covering the whole country, while North Wales Rover tickets allow one day's travel on buses and trains in various zones across North Wales (www.tfw.wales). Red Rover bus tickets offer a day's unlimited travel in Gwynedd and Anglesey, some services in Conwy, and Snowdon Sherpa bus travel. For

Going green

Snowdonia has an excellent network of buses, including the Snowdon Sherpa, a circular service around the northern part of the region giving access to the mountains and main towns (Apr–Sep), the point being to reduce the number of cars on the roads in the National Park: www.snowdonia.gov.wales. Regional services across Anglesey, through the Vale of Conwy, down the Cardigan Bay coast and inland to Machynlleth, provide a relaxed and 'green' way to enjoy the scenery. Combined with bus routes, narrow-gauge railways and with some careful planning, much of Snowdonia is accessible without a car.

Strolling along the Anglesey coastal path at Porth Trecastell.

Snowdonia for children

Few places in Britain have such an abundance of visitor attractions as Snowdonia. Most of these are suitable for children of a range of ages and have been described in the main Places section of this guide. They include the region's Great Little Trains (see Tours 3, 4, 7 and 9); its slate caverns at Blaenau Ffestiniog (see page 47), and its many historical museums. Then there are all the castles, King Arthur's Labyrinth (see page 93) and the Centre for Alternative Technology (see page 94) – the list goes on.

For information on self-guided walks suitable for families, call into one of the Snowdonia National Park information centres. Most mountain-bike hire centres cater for youngsters and will provide guidance on which trails are suitable. Traditional longbow archery, woodland den building, and donkey riding are some of the activities at the Greenwood Forest Park near Caernarfon, tel: 01248 670076.

enquiries about public transport in Gwynedd, visit www.gwynedd. llyw.cymru/en, or across Wales, www.traveline.cymru. For tourist steam trains visit www.greatlittletrains ofwales.co.uk. Between April and September, the Sherpa'r Wyddfa bus runs various routes around the base of Snowdon, allowing walkers and climbers to hop on and off as they wish, www.sherparwydffa.wales.

By car
Having a car does give you the flexibility to visit the hidden corners of Snowdonia. Car hire is available in Cardiff from various operators, in Llandudno from Avis (www.avis. co.uk), and in Aberystwyth, Anglesey Airport and Caernarfon from Europcar (www.europcar.co.uk).

Cycling
Snowdonia is becoming increasingly easy to explore by bike, with many recreational cycle routes, such as the Mawddach Trail, a 9-mile (14km) route from Dolgellau to Morfa Mawddach, and trails in Coed-y-brenin. There are mountain-bike trails

and easy forestry tracks – SNP visitor centres have information. Bikes can be hired from locations such as Beics Betws in Betws-y-coed, www.bike wales.co.uk and Dolgellau Cycles in Dolgellau, www.dolgellaucycles.co.uk.

Facts for the visitor

Accessible travel
Much accommodation in Snowdonia is in older buildings or smaller B&Bs, so lifts are not standard. However, they will be present in larger chain hotels. Always check access on booking and note that some accommodation providers have specially adapted rooms. For information on the best places to stay with disabled access, visit www.goodaccessguide.co.uk. While public railways and buses have access and wheelchair areas, small stations may be unstaffed and lifts may be closed, so check before travelling. Tourism for All provides general information and contacts, www.tourismforall.co.uk. Information for travel within the UK for visitors with disabilities can also be found at www.gov.uk/transport-disabled.

The Snowdonia National Park website (www.snowdonia.gov.wales, see under Snowdonia for all) has a section devoted to accessible travel in the region, with details of easy-access car parks and toilets. They also have a programme of countryside wheelchair walks, posted on their website, and guided monthly walks aimed at visually impaired travellers (tel: 01745 827990). Ableworld (www.ableworld. co.uk) have shops in Rhyl (tel: 01745 336843) and Llandudno (tel: 01492 338549), and offer wheelchair and mobility scooter hire.

Emergencies
Dial 999 and ask the operator for the appropriate service: Police, Ambulance,

A good map and compass are essential for walking in Snowdonia.

Fire Brigade, Coastguard or Mountain Rescue. (NB: mountain rescue call-outs are initiated by the Police.)

LGBTQ+ travellers
There are LGBTQ+ communities in North Wales, but the liveliest scene is in the south in Cardiff. Visit Wales (www.visitwales.com) has a section of information on LGBTQ+ friendly Wales, focusing on Cardiff, including places to stay and LGBTQ+ clubs and bars. Aberystwyth has the reputation of being Wales's most LGBTQ+ friendly town.

Maps
Ordnance Survey Explorer maps 1:25,000 cover Snowdon and Conwy Valley areas (Sheet OL 17), Harlech and

Preparing the miniature train at Betws-y-coed.

Snowdonia souvenirs

Traditional crafts can be found in numerous outlets throughout Snowdonia. Carved to make gifts and useful items, slate is a popular souvenir; it is available at craft shops and at such visitor attractions as the Inigo Jones Slateworks near Caernarfon and Blaenau Ffestiniog's slate mines. Portmeirion pottery is well regarded and widely collected; it can be purchased from Portmeirion and other quality gift shops.

Local potteries, some part of co-operatives, abound in north Wales.

Bala areas (Sheet OL 18) and Cadair Idris area (Sheet OL 23). In addition, you may need Explorer 262, 263 (which cover Anglesey), and 253 and 254 (which cover the Lleyn Peninsula).

Opening hours

Standard business hours are Mon–Fri 9am–5pm or 5.30pm; post offices will also open Sat 9am–noon. Shop core hours are Mon–Sat 9am–5.30pm. In larger towns like Caernarfon, some shops may stay open later, especially in peak season – they may also open on Sunday between 10am and 4pm.

Tourist information

For more information about visiting Snowdonia, contact either a National

The heraldic dragon is the Welsh national symbol.

Park Centre or a local Tourist Information Centre (TIC)

Snowdonia National Park (SNP) Head Office, Penrhyndeudraeth; www.snowdonia.gov.wales; National Park Centres: Aberdyfi, tel: 01654 767321; Beddgelert, tel: 01766 890615; Betws-y-coed, tel: 01690 710426.

Tourist Information Centres contain a wide range of leaflets and publications, many of them free. In addition to answering public transport enquiries, staff can usually assist with accommodation bookings. Suggestions for eating out, places to visit and details of local events are also offered.

Beddgelert: Yr Hen Gapel, tel: 01766 890615; Conwy: Rose Hill Street, tel: 01492 577566; Llanberis: Hwb Eryri, Electric Mountain, tel: 01286 870500; Llandudno: Victoria Centre, Mostyn Street, tel: 01492 577577; Llangollen: Y Capel, Castle Street, tel: 01978 860828; Rhyl: The Village, West Parade, tel: 01745 355068; Wrexham: Lambit Street, tel: 01978 292015.

Go North Wales, www.gonorthwales. co.uk; Visit Wales, www.visitwales.com; Visit Snowdonia, www.visitsnowdonia. info; The Isle of Anglesey, www.visit anglesey.co.uk; North East Wales, www.northeastwales.wales.

Accommodation

Snowdonia and North Wales have a wide selection of serviced accommodation, ranging from clean, modest guesthouses to boutique and luxury hotels with every amenity. Many establishments serve dinner as an optional extra and there may also be special reductions for children. TICs hold details of local accommodation, and most will help with bookings.

The area also has a great choice of good-value, self-catering cottages, farmhouses, flats, chalets and static caravans. One specialist self-catering agency is Wales Cottage Holidays (Bear Lanes, Newtown, Powys; www.walescottageholidays.co.uk). Snowdonia also has many excellent campsites, costing between £12 and £20 for an overnight pitch.

You could go back to nature and stay in a tipi or a yurt at Eco Retreats (www.ecoretreats.co.uk), a few miles northeast of Machynlleth. There's no electricity and eco-friendliness is a priority.

The Youth Hostel Association (www.yha.org.uk) has bunkhouses and hostels throughout Snowdonia. To book, call the individual hostel, or telephone 0800 019 1700.

The price codes listed are based on a standard double for one night in peak season, including breakfast. Out of season prices can be much lower and many establishments offer special deals, so check websites before booking.

£££ = over £150
££ = £100–150
£ = under £100

Ruthin and the Vale of Clywd

Bach y Graig Farmhouse
Tremeirchion, St Asaph;
www.bachygraig.co.uk.

Wooden beams, oak panelling and an inglenook fireplace impart plenty of character to this farmhouse B&B. There are free-range eggs and freshly baked bread for breakfast. Self-catering accommodation is also available. Adults only. £

Castle House
Bull Lane, Denbigh;
www.castlehousebandb.co.uk.
Situated in the grounds of Leicester's Folly just below the castle, the three supremely comfortable rooms and two cottages here come with ornate furnishings and stunning views. Guest's lounge and gardens to enjoy too. ££

Firgrove
Llanfwrog, Ruthin;
www.firgrovecountryhouse.co.uk.
Beautifully furnished bedrooms at this charming Georgian house, just on the outskirts of Ruthin. The large gardens are well maintained and create a tranquil setting. Two-night minimum stay. ££

Manorhaus
Well Street, Ruthin; www.manorhaus.com/ruthin.
Wonderfully stylish bedrooms and cool modern artworks characterise this excellent restaurant with rooms, situated in a Georgian building. Comfort isn't sacrificed to style, and there are fluffy towels, Egyptian cotton bed linen and sleek bathrooms. £

Pentre Mawr
Llandyrnog, nr Denbigh; www.unusualweddingvenueswales.co.uk.
This country house looks traditional, but contains some surprises: you can stay in classic rooms with four-poster beds in the house itself, or opt for luxurious safari-style canvas lodges in the grounds which come with underfloor heating, rich fabrics and

Escape B&B, Llandudno.

hot tubs. Dinner is available on Friday and Saturday. £££

Llandudno

Bodysgallen Hall and Spa
2 miles (3km) outside Llandudno; www.bodysgallen.com.
Luxury all the way at this fine country-house hotel, owned by the National Trust. There's a spa, and fabulous gardens, as well as an elegant restaurant. £££

Escape Boutique B&B
48 Church Walks; www.escapebandb.co.uk.
It may be a Victorian villa, but this stylish B&B has contemporary individually designed rooms, bringing welcome urban chic to Llandudno. Retro and vintage furnishings and all kinds of curios add to its considerable charm. ££

The Lighthouse
Marine Drive; www.lighthouse-llandudno.co.uk.
You get great sea views from this B&B, situated in a nineteenth-century lighthouse which was built to resemble a fortress. It's perched on Great Orme Head, a couple of miles from Llandudno. £

The Wildings
North Parade, Promenade; www.thewildlingshotel.co.uk.
Traditionally decorated, comfortable bedrooms at this luxurious small hotel on the seafront. Alice Liddell – immortalised as Alice in Wonderland – stayed here as a child, and it retains a sense of Victorian grandeur. Lovely sea views from the lounge and excellent food in the restaurant. £

Vale of Conwy and Conwy

Castle Hotel
High Street, Conwy; www.castlewales.co.uk.
Once a coaching inn, this centrally-located hotel mixes period features, like wood panelling and old beams, with refurbished boutique bedrooms. It serves fine Welsh food in the restaurant. ££

Glan Heulog
Llanwrst Road, Conwy; www.conwy-bedandbreakfast.co.uk.
A warm reception awaits at this delightful guesthouse with six ensuite rooms, including a family room. Breakfast is taken in the light-filled conservatory. Half a mile out of town on the Trefriw Road. ££

The Quay Hotel and Spa
Deganwy Quay, Deganwy;
www.quayhotel.co.uk.
Contemporary-styled rooms and suites
at this waterfront hotel with a spa and
swimming pool. Many rooms have
great views of Conwy castle – you can
even go for a penthouse with your own
balcony. £££

Around Betws-y-Coed and Snowdon

Ffin y Parc Country House
Betws Road, Llanrwst;
www.welshart.net.
Two luxury self-catering cottages
set in the grounds of a stone-built
country house with a Victorian
walled garden. Style is eclectic, with
a mix of antique and contemporary
furnishings. £££

Pen y Gwryd Hotel
Nant Gwynant; www.pyg.co.uk.
This traditional inn, a one-time base
for Everest expedition training, attracts
plenty of walkers and climbers who
want clean, no-frills accommodation
with good food. £–££

Pengwern Country House
Allt Dinas, nr Betws-y-Coed;
www.snowdonia
accommodation.co.uk.
Friendly Welsh-speaking hosts and
immaculate rooms set in a Victorian
house just a mile (1.6km) from the
centre of Betws-y-Coed. The rooms
are individually designed – the
Richard Gay Somerset bathroom
offers the best loo-with-a-view in
Wales. £

St Curig's Church
Capel Curig;
www.stcurigschurch.com.
You'll find this converted nineteenth-
century church a comfortable
self-catering option. It's popular
with walkers and climbers. Choose
from en-suite rooms, twin beds and
bunkrooms. £££

Swallow Falls Inn
Holyhead Road, Betws-y-Coed;
www.inncollectiongroup.com.
A convenient base for lovers of the
great outdoors. The inn has 19 en-
suite bedrooms, and there's also a
neighbouring campsite and YHA
hostel. There's home-cooked food in
the Tavern Restaurant or pub bar, and
landscaped gardens beside the famous
Swallow Falls waterfall. £

Ceiriog Valley

The Hand at Llanarmon
Llanarmon Dyffryn Ceiriog;
www.thehandhotel.co.uk.
The beautiful Ceiriog Valley is the
setting for this former farm which
is now a popular hotel. There are
guest rooms in the farmhouse and in
converted outbuildings, and excellent
food is served in the restaurant. ££

Anglesey

Bishopsgate Hotel & Restaurant
Castle Street, Beaumaris;
www.bishopsgatehotel.co.uk.
Bishopgate Hotel, located in a lovely
restored Georgian townhouse, has
nine individually designed rooms. The
public areas are tastefully decorated
and feature antique furnishings and
original features. There's an excellent,
award-winning restaurant, too. £

Bull's Head Inn
Castle Street, Beaumaris;
www.inncollectiongroup.co.uk.
This historic coaching inn, where
Charles Dickens once stayed, has five
cosy bedrooms, many with original
features. If you prefer funkier, more
contemporary rooms, you can stay in
the stylish Townhouse – a former inn,
also on Castle Street. ££

Lastra Farm Hotel
Penrhyd, Amlwch; www.lastra-
hotel.co.uk.
In a good position for visiting the
island, Lastra Farm is a comfortable,

Portmeirion Hotel

Portmeirion and Ffestiniog

Portmeirion Hotel and Castell Deudraeth
Portmeirion; www.portmeirion.wales.
There are two hotels at Portmeirion, both offering luxurious accommodation in the magical setting of this Italianate village, as well as self-catering cottages and 'village rooms'. £££

Tyddyn du Farm
Gellilydan, Ffestiniog, nr Porthmadog; www.snowdoniaholidays.wales.
This working sheep farm has high-quality accommodation in spacious barn suites sleeping two- to five people and all with countryside views. ££

Aberdyfi

Awel y Mor
4, Bodfor Terrace, Aberdyfi; www.awel-y-mor-bedabndbreakfast.co.uk.
Seafront-facing *Awel y Mar* offers four attractively appointed rooms (all en-suite), two of which have spectacular views, in addition to a ground floor self-catering apartment. £

friendly establishment whose clientele keep on returning. The restaurant (closed Mon & Tues) uses local suppliers for its seafood, meat and vegetables. £

Lleyn Peninsula

Gwesty Ty Newydd
Aberdaron; www.gwesty-tynewydd.co.uk.
There are great sea views from all eleven bedrooms of this attractive inn, situated beside the beach. Two rooms have been adapted for guests with disabilities, and there's a popular seafood restaurant downstairs. ££

Porth Tocyn
Abersoch; www.porthtocynhotel.co.uk.
Some two miles south of the village, this ever so smart country house hotel offers uniquely styled rooms, most of which have outstanding views of Cardigan Bay. Self-catering cottage and shepherd's hut too. £££

Southern Snowdonia

Graig Wen
Arthog, Dolgellau; www.graigwen.co.uk.
Five miles west of Dolgellau, this fabulous retreat incorporates wild camping, yurts, bell tents, two quarry wagons and a quartet of self-catering cottages. Pitches for motorhomes too. £

Tyddyn Mawr Farmhouse
Cader Road, Dolgellau; www.wales-guesthouse.co.uk.
There are two bedrooms at this five-star B&B outside Dolgellau. One room has great views of Cadair Idris, the other has access onto the patio. A cracking Welsh breakfast is served in the farmhouse. £

Index

Credits

Pocket Rough Guide Snowdonia and North Wales Weekender
Editor: Rachel Lawrence, Lizzie Horrocks
Author: Rebecca Ford
Picture Manager: Tom Smyth
Cartography: Katie Bennett
Head of DTP and Pre-Press: Rebeka Davies
Head of Publishing: Sarah Clark
Photo credits: Alamy 13T; Alan Harris 26; Arwel Parry 15B; Cadwalader's Café 13B; Crown Copyright 6BL, 7CR, 7BR, 8/9, 9B, 24T, 38/39, 63, 110/111, 114, 126; Denis Egan 119; Fotolia 30/31, 31, 32, 33, 34, 35, 55T, 81T, 85T, 97, 100, 113; Gary Pollmiller 15T; Getty Images 58T; Hafod Eryri 57T, 57B; Ian Parkes 41T; iStock 6BR, 22/23, 28, 38TL, 48, 75T, 77T, 77B, 78T, 81B, 115, 121T; James West 93T; Mark Rowland 116; Mike Bean 104; Public domain 68B, 73T, 95B, 103B; Shutterstock 1, 4/5, 6TL, 7TL, 7TR, 7CL, 10, 14, 38B, 50, 58B, 59, 62, 75B, 84T, 85B, 86, 88B, 88/89, 96T, 102B, 103T, 112; Stemonitis 25T; William Shaw/Apa Publications 7BL, 11B, 11T, 16, 18T, 18B, 19, 20B, 20T, 21T, 21B, 23, 24B, 25B, 29T, 29B, 36T, 36B, 37, 40, 41B, 42B, 42T, 44B, 44T, 45, 46, 47, 51, 52, 53T, 53B, 54T, 54B, 55B, 56, 60R, 61, 64B, 65T, 65, 66B, 66T, 67T, 67B, 68T, 70, 71, 72, 73B, 74, 76, 78B, 80, 82, 83, 84B, 88TL, 91, 92B, 92T, 93B, 94, 95T, 96B, 98, 101, 102T, 105B, 105T, 106T, 106B, 107, 108B, 108T, 117T, 117B, 118, 120, 121B, 122T, 122B, 124
Cover credits: Snowdon peak from lake Llynnau Mymbyr Shutterstock

Contact Us

Every effort has been made to provide accurate information in this publication, but changes are inevitable. The publisher cannot be held responsible for any resulting loss, inconvenience or injury sustained by any traveller as a result of information or advice contained in the guide. We would appreciate it if readers would call our attention to any errors or outdated information, or if you feel we've left something out. Please send your comments with the subject line "**Pocket Rough Guide Snowdonia and North Wales Weekender Update**" to mail@uk.roughguides.com.

First edition 2024

Printed in Czech Republic

Contains Land-Form Panorama Contours & Meridian 2 and OS Street View data © Crown copyright and database right.

Distribution

UK, Ireland and Europe: Apa Publications (UK) Ltd; sales@roughguides.com
United States and Canada: Ingram Publisher Services; ips@ingramcontent.com
Australia and New Zealand: Booktopia; retailer@booktopia.com.au
Worldwide: Apa Publications (UK) Ltd; sales@roughguides.com

Special Sales, Content Licensing and CoPublishing

Rough Guides can be purchased in bulk quantities at discounted prices. We can create special editions, personalised jackets and corporate imprints tailored to your needs. sales@roughguides.com; http://roughguides.com